PRAYERS FOR THE DAY

PRAYERS FOR THE DAY

Contemporary Collects

Frederick W. Kemper

Publishing House
St. Louis

Concordia Publishing House, St. Louis, Missouri
Copyright © 1980, Concordia Publishing House

MANUFACTURED IN THE UNITED STATES OF AMERICA

Library of Congress Cataloging in Publication Data

Kemper, Frederick W
    Prayers for the day.

      1. Collects. 2. Church year—Prayer-books and devotions—English. I. Title.
BV30.K43   264'.041013   80-10403
ISBN 0-570-03070-6

Dedicated to
the bride of Christ
in and for
whose service
these prayers
were written

Foreword

The collects in this book are presented to give more precise unity to the variable parts of the liturgical service. The prayer should match the message.

The three-year cycle of pericopes offers a far greater variety of preaching texts than the one-year series. It therefore calls for a wider variety of prayers. Here a collect is offered for each Epistle and for each Old Testament and Gospel combination in the three-year cycle. All the collects for a given Sunday are printed as a group, but they are divided according to their application to series A, B, and C of the lessons.

It is my quiet prayer that the collects presented here prove useful to the church, but more, it is my fervent prayer that God be praised and God's people be blessed and guided by the praying of them.

FWK

Contents

Collects for the Church Year

Collects for the Lesser Festivals

Collects for Special Occasions

Collects for the Church Year

First Sunday in Advent

Lesson II: Romans 13:11-14

Holy Spirit, who sanctifies and keeps us in the saving faith, keep the vision and excitement of Christ's coming to us and for us so alive in us that we constantly acquit ourselves as people ready for His appearing; through Jesus Christ, our Lord, who with You and the Father are one God with dominion over us forever.

Lesson I: Isaiah 2:1-5
The Gospel: Matthew 24:37-44; or Matthew 21:1-11

Fill us with anticipation, activate our hope, O Son of God and Son of Man, who having redeemed us at Your first advent, has promised to come again in the fullness of time, in radiant splendor, to lead us into eternal glory; who with the Father and the Holy Spirit are one God with dominion over us forever.

B

Lesson II: 1 Corinthians 1:3-9

By deepening our understanding of where we are between the first and second advents of our Christ, excite us to endless alleluias, O Holy Spirit of God, that we may be moved to thanksgiving, to prayer and praise, and to joyous living in our anticipation of the end-time event; through Jesus Christ, our Lord, who with You and the Father are one God with dominion over us forever.

Lesson I: Isaiah 63:16b-17; 64:1-8
The Gospel: Mark 13:33-37 or Mark 11:1-10

King of kings, whose return in splendor at the end-time is a bulwark of our faith, give us patience to wait and watch and listen for the first sounds of the herald trumpets, because we are excited beyond our ability to contain it with wanting Your return; who with the Father and the Holy Spirit are one God with dominion over us forever.

C

Lesson II: 1 Thessalonians 3:9-13

Lord Jesus, surrounded by saints and angels, help us to overcome our selfishness that our hearts may be blameless before God, our Father, and our lives increase and abound in love to one another and to all people, until You come with all Your saints and angels to take us home; who with the Father and the Holy Spirit are one God with dominion over us forever.

Lesson I: Jeremiah 33:14-16
The Gospel: Luke 21:25-36 or Luke 19:28-40

Our excitement leaps unbounded, heavenly Father, Giver of every good and perfect gift, for Your unspeakable generosity which assures us peace in time and hope for all eternity in our Lord, Jesus Christ; through the same Jesus Christ, our Lord, who with You and the Holy Spirit are one God with dominion over us forever.

Second Sunday in Advent

A

Lesson II: Romans 15:4-13

For the hope burning in us, for the joy and peace You have given us in Christ by the power of the Spirit, O God, we rejoice in You, we praise You, we sing Your name before all the world; through Jesus Christ, our Lord, who with You and the Holy Spirit are one God with dominion over us forever.

Lesson I: Isaiah 11:1-10
The Gospel: Matthew 3:1-12

Holy Spirit, by whose power and choosing John the Baptist called people to repentance and announced to them the imminence of the kingdom of Christ in his day, give to us to whom the Kingdom has come a ready willingness to announce the accomplishment of Christ to our world that You and that Kingdom might claim all people of our time as well; through Jesus Christ our Lord, who with You and the Father are one God with dominion over us forever.

B

Lesson II: 2 Peter 3:8-14

Let us so believe and trust, Son of Man and Son of God, that the excitement and wonder of Your return to our small planet to claim Your people for the New Jerusalem in regal pomp and radiant splendor will mightily exceed our anticipation of that end-time event, and so justify our eager waiting and our certain hope; who with the Father and the Holy Spirit are one God with dominion over us forever.

Lesson I: Isaiah 40:1-11
The Gospel: Mark 1:1-8

Excite us by Your promises made and fulfilled in Jesus Christ, and all fulfillment still to come, almighty God, that we have humility enough to bow in repentance for our sins, faith enough to live in Your forgiveness, and hope enough, born of Your promises, to maintain us until Jesus comes in glory; who with You and the Holy Spirit are one God with dominion over us forever.

C

Lesson II: Philippians 1:3-11

Holy Spirit, who makes saints out of sinners through the redemption of Jesus, the Christ, fill us with the fruits of righteousness which come through Jesus Christ, that our sinner-self may come more nearly to match our sainthood in the waiting time till Christ's return; through the same Jesus Christ, our Lord, who with You and the Father are one God with dominion over us forever.

Lesson I: Malachi 3:1-4
The Gospel: Luke 3:1-6

Heavenly Father, whose will is that all people be saved, for the heralds of the past and the proclaimers of the Good News in the present we ask Your blessing, that the power of the Spirit move all who hear them to accept Your Son in faith, and so fulfill Your heart's desire; through Jesus Christ, our Lord, who with You and the Holy Spirit are one God with dominion over us forever.

Third Sunday in Advent

===== A =====

Lesson II: James 5:7-10

Lord of the end-time testing, grant patience to Your church and to all of us its people against Your announced arrival time to judge the world; through Jesus Christ, our Redeemer, who with You and the Holy Spirit are one God with dominion over us forever.

Lesson I: Isaiah 35:1-10
The Gospel: Matthew 11:2-11

We lift high our hearts before the eternal God, O Holy Spirit, Comforter of God's people, for through You in the ever-present Christ the fainthearted find new courage, the weary discover the Burden-Bearer, and the broken discover healing and peace; through Jesus Christ, our Lord, who with You and the Father are one God with dominion over us forever.

===== B =====

Lesson II: 1 Thessalonians 5:16-24

Eternal Judge, whose mercy and grace in Jesus Christ effected our release from condemnation and filled us with the hope of the end-time glory, help us to live rejoicing, praying, obeying the Spirit, abhorring evil, and seeking good, and keep us sanctified, sound, and blameless until Christ comes; through Jesus Christ, our Lord, who with You and the Holy Spirit are one God with dominion over us forever.

Lesson I: Isaiah 61:1-3, 10-11
The Gospel: John 1:6-8, 19-28

Holy Spirit, Keeper of the mystery, grant us to recognize Jesus of

Nazareth for who and what He is, lest we become only debating pupils rather than selfless disciples calling the world to repentance and faith; through Jesus Christ, our Lord, who with You and the Father are one God with dominion over us forever.

C

Lesson II: Philippians 4:4-7 (8-9)

Gracious, omnipotent Lord, whose throne room is open to us and who hears our prayers, forgive us when we doubt Your concern and wonder where You are, and teach us to rejoice in Your constant presence in the midst of the trying and the easy times of living; through Jesus Christ, our Lord, who with You and the Holy Spirit are one God with dominion over us forever.

Lesson I
Zephaniah 3:14-18a (" . . . day of festival.")
The Gospel: Luke 3:7-18

Almighty God, who holds the destiny of every person and the ultimate resolution of all created things in Your hand, restrain us from hypocrisy, maintain us in integrity, and keep us in our joy that Christ has come and will come again; through the same Jesus Christ, our Lord, who with You and the Holy Spirit are one God with dominion over us forever.

Fourth Sunday in Advent

A

Lesson II: Romans 1:1-7

Our hearts are high, our joy is full, beloved Jesus Christ, who died and rose again for the justification of all people, because we are included in those who have been called to belong to You and because the same possibility is available to all mankind; who with the Father and the Holy Spirit are one God with dominion over us forever.

Lesson I: Isaiah 7:10-14 (15-17)
The Gospel: Matthew 1:18-25

Heavenly Father, whose ways are past finding out, we are greatly moved and mightily excited that Your plan for the salvation for the world, conceived in deep Trinitarian council, became visible in the little Child of Bethlehem that we might better understand the plan's unfolding and its end; through Jesus Christ, our Lord, who with You and the Holy Spirit are one God with dominion over us forever.

B

Lesson II: Romans 16:25-27

Glory be to You, eternal Father, for expounding the mystery through Your prophets and evangelists of the advent of Your Christ for our salvation, by which our eternity has been assured when He comes again in all His glorious splendor for us; through the same Jesus Christ, our Lord, who with You and the Holy Spirit are one God with dominion over us forever.

Lesson I: 2 Samuel 7:(1-7) 8-11, 16
The Gospel: Luke 1:26-38

Omniscient Father, whose mind and heart conceived the plan of redemption, for the consummate care and profound judgment involving archangels, ordinary angels, special people, but beyond all else Your Son for carrying out the plan, our grateful thanks and a mighty prayer that we whom You have judged worthy of carrying the Good News to our peers be most reliable in the responsibility You have given us; through Jesus Christ, our Lord, who with You and the Holy Spirit are one God with dominion over us forever.

C

Lesson II: Hebrews 10:5-10

Eternal God, who in the Son has offered Yourself as the last great Sacrifice for us, and who in the Spirit has sanctified us because of it, raise our hearts in praise and thanksgiving until we are called to the Father's mansions; through Jesus Christ, our Lord, who with You and the Holy Spirit are one God with dominion over us forever.

Lesson I: Micah 5:2-4
The Gospel: Luke 1:39-45 (46-55)

Omnipotent Lord, who in Your good time set into motion the plan for our redemption, help us to appreciate the mighty miracles through which the last of the old covenant prophets and the Christ are established on the course to effect our redemption and reconciliation with You; through Jesus Christ, our Lord, who with You and the Holy Spirit are one God with dominion over us forever.

The Nativity of Our Lord
Christmas Day

A

Lesson II: Titus 2:11-14

God of all grace, who has accomplished our salvation, help us always to remember the first appearance of Your Christ with thanksgiving and to hope with fervent expectation for His final coming; through Jesus Christ, our Lord, who with You and the Holy Spirit are one God with dominion over us forever.

Lesson I: Isaiah 9:2-7
The Gospel: Luke 2:1-20

King of kings, Lord of lords, Center of the Father's plan for our salvation, Focal-Point for all history, Ruler of all the universe, for having come to us, for coming to us still, for the end-time coming for us, we say our prayers of joyous thanksgiving and praise You, who are beyond and above all things, on this day of celebration of Your incarnation; who with the Father and the Holy Spirit are one God with dominion over us forever.

B

Lesson II: Hebrews 1:1-9

Excite us to song and praise this birth day of the Christ whose gift of the Holy Spirit brought us to faith, causes us to love, and sustains us by hope of His appearing, dear Heavenly Father, that You may know our gratitude for Your gift; through Jesus Christ, our Lord, who with You and the Holy Spirit are one God with dominion over us forever.

Lesson I: Isaiah 52:7-10
The Gospel: John 1:1-14

Eternal Father, whose Christmas presence is the best of all gifts, for the quiet Word of Bethlehem, for the loving Word in ministry, for the mighty Word of Calvary, for the affirming Word of Easter and for the quiet Word that fills us and causes us to glorify and praise You this day of celebration, we thank You; through Jesus Christ, our Lord, who with You and the Holy Spirit are one God with dominion over us forever.

C

Lesson II: Titus 3:4-7

Because we have been adopted into Your family with all its exciting benefits, beloved Father of our Lord Jesus Christ and our Father, give us the spirit of wisdom to love all the saints in the holy communion and all people in the family of man and to pray that they may all share in the hope and inheritance to which we have been called; through Jesus Christ, our Lord, who with You and the Holy Spirit are one God with dominion over us forever.

Lesson I: Isaiah 62:10-12
The Gospel: Luke 2:1-20

Eternal Word, who full of grace and truth was made flesh to dwell among us, fill us with Yourself and with faith that we may be heralds ceaselessly proclaiming the Word to the world; who with the Father and the Holy Spirit are one God with dominion over us forever.

First Sunday After Christmas

Lesson II: Galatians 4:4-7

Heavenly Father, gracious Lord, forgive us for ever offending You, for our adoption out of our slavery to the world and from the tyranny of our own flesh into Your holy family is our highest and most cherished possession; through Jesus Christ, our Lord, who with You and the Holy Spirit are one God with dominion over us forever.

Lesson I: Isaiah 63:7-9

The Gospel: Matthew 2:13-15, 19-23

Heavenly Father, into whose tender hands we have placed ourselves for shelter from all that would hurt us, assure us that every misfortune we suffer comes to us with Your full knowledge that we may endure it with fortitude and dignity for Your sake; through Jesus Christ, our Lord, who with You and the Holy Spirit are one God with dominion over us forever.

Lesson II: Colossians 3:12-17

Blessed God, Father to Christ and to us, adorn us through Your Holy Spirit with proper life and living as becomes those who have seen the Christ and believed, as an expression of our gratitude to You for so profound a Gift; through the same Jesus Christ, our Lord, who with You and the Holy Spirit are one God with dominion over us forever.

Lesson I: Isaiah 45:22-25

The Gospel: Luke 2:25-40

Glorious and gracious Christ, who knows the Father's judgment against us, who came to us to redeem us by dying on Calvary's cross, maintain our faith that we may daily stand ready to die for You; who with the Father and the Holy Spirit are one God with dominion over us forever.

C

Lesson II: Hebrews 2:10-18

Incarnate Son of God, Pioneer of our salvation, who took on our flesh to suffer and die to expiate our sins and lead us to glory, strengthen us in our resolve, born of Your example, as we who are Your family seek to care for each other and for all whom You came to redeem; who with the Father and the Holy Spirit are one God with dominion over us forever.

Lesson I: Jeremiah 31:10-13
The Gospel: Luke 2:41-52

Gracious heavenly Father, who sent Your Son into our world to redeem it from its sin, give us a mind that searches for Your revealed truth and a will to be continually about Your business, for Your mercy in the gift of Christ to us requires no less from us; through Jesus Christ, our Lord, who with You and the Holy Spirit are one God with dominion over us forever.

Second Sunday After Christmas

A, B, C

Lesson II: Ephesians 1:3-6, 15-18

Heavenly Father, gracious Lord, by whose Christ we have been elected to Your holy family, give us a spirit of wisdom and revelation and an appreciation of the rich inheritance He has promised, that we order our lives in love toward all saints and sinners; through Jesus Christ, our Lord, who with You and the Holy Spirit are one God with dominion over us forever.

Or

Heavenly Father, from whose loving hand blessing after blessing has been heaped upon us, we offer our deepest thanks for Christ, for faith, for adoption, for the Spirit, and for hope; through Jesus Christ, our Lord, who with You and the Holy Spirit are one God with dominion over us forever.

Or

Because we have been adopted into Your family with all its exciting benefits, beloved Father of our Lord Jesus Christ, give us the spirit of wisdom to love all the saints in the holy communion and all the people in the family of mankind, for we shall share in the hope and inheritance to which we have been called; through Jesus Christ, our Lord, who with You and the Holy Spirit are one God with dominion over us forever.

Lesson I: Isaiah 61:10—62:3
The Gospel: John 1:1-18

Eternal Word, made flesh to dwell among us full of grace and truth, fill us with the Word and with faith, for we must be heralds making proclamation of the Word to the world; who with the

24

Father and the Holy Spirit are one God with dominion over us forever.

Or

All-knowing, all-powerful Lord, from whom come our most treasured gifts, we thank You for the Word, the Light, and the life You have given us, and we pray Your blessing on us that we hear Him, follow Him, and live for Him in this world; through the same Jesus Christ, our Lord, who with You and the Holy Spirit are one God with dominion over us forever.

Or

Holy Word, glorious Light, Infant of Bethlehem, ruling Lord, give us ears to hear You reveal the justice and love of God, our Father, and grace to walk in the splendor of Your glory; who with the Father and the Holy Spirit are one God with dominion over us forever.

Epiphany

Lesson II: Ephesians 3:2-12

Gracious and loving Father, whose love has superseded justice and who purposed in love to redeem the world, we praise You for revealing the mystery of the cross and the Christ to us, for our salvation depends on our knowing and accepting His death and resurrection for us, through Jesus Christ, our Lord, who with You and the Holy Spirit are one God with dominion over us forever.

Or

Holy Spirit, Promoter of the Kingdom, Dispenser of the holy faith, because You have disclosed the mystery of Christ to us, and caught us into it, use us to proclaim Him, that the Kingdom of Grace prosper to the good of the human family and the glory of the King; through Jesus Christ, our Lord, who with You and the Father are one God with dominion over us forever.

Lesson I: Isaiah 60:1-6
The Gospel: Matthew 2:1-12

God of love, who would like to see the salvation of all, keep us steadfast in the faith and use us to preach to all—in this way let people find salvation for their souls, and then let them, lighted with Christ's light, glorify You; through Jesus Christ, our Lord, who with You and the Holy Spirit are one God with dominion over us forever.

Or

Blessed Redeemer, to whom the Wise Men came offering gifts, fill our minds and hearts with Jesus, guide our life and living for Jesus, and take us at last into glory where at Your throne we can lay before You our praise and honor as our grateful tribute; who with the Father and the Holy Spirit are one God with dominion over us forever.

The Baptism of Our Lord
First Sunday After the Epiphany

A

Lesson II: Acts 10:34-38

Heavenly Father, before whom all the universe must bow, since in Jesus Christ, Your Son, You set the ultimate example of obedience and service to the world, and since through our baptism into Christ's death and resurrection You have set us into ministry to our neighbor, give us direction and strength for similar obedient service; through Jesus Christ, our Lord, who with You and the Holy Spirit are one God with dominion over us forever.

Lesson I: Isaiah 42:1-7
The Gospel: Matthew 3:13-17

Blessed Trinity, who has given us so much, strengthen us who in Baptism have committed ourselves to You, that we, following Your example, empty ourselves in service to all who are in need of our help; through Jesus Christ, our Lord, who with the Father and the Holy Spirit are one God with dominion over us forever.

B

Lesson II: Acts 10:34-38

Holy, heavenly Father, who shows no partiality to anyone, Accepter of all who come to You in Jesus Christ, keep our eyes on Him, that we in similar impartiality proclaim the Good News to all who will listen; through Jesus Christ, our Lord, who with You and the Holy Spirit are one God with dominion over us forever.

Lesson I: Isaiah 42:1-7
The Gospel: Mark 1:4-11

Holy and blessed Trinity—Creator, Redeemer, Sanctifier—since our baptism washed away our sin, guaranteed us lambs of the Good Shepherd, and ordained us priests, keep us in mind of our baptism lest we lose the blessings given to us in it; who are one God with dominion over us forever.

═══════════ **C** ═══════════

Lesson II: Acts 10:34-38

Holy Spirit, whose desire is to confront the whole world with Jesus Christ, who died for it in perfect obedience to the Father, who loved it, use us as You will to fulfill Your desire; who with Jesus Christ, our Lord, and the Father are one God with dominion over us forever.

Lesson I: Isaiah 42:1-7
The Gospel: Luke 3:15-17; 21-22

Gracious heavenly Father, who in awesome voice presented Your beloved Son and obedient Servant to the world at the Jordan baptism, use our weak voices and faltering lives to identify Christ, our Lord, as every person's Savior from damnation and as mankind's only way back to You and to the eternal mansions; through Jesus Christ, our Lord, who with You and the Holy Spirit are one God with dominion over us forever.

Second Sunday After the Epiphany

Lesson II: 1 Corinthians 1:1-9

Faithful God and Father, who by the Holy Spirit has called us into fellowship with Jesus Christ, enriched us with the Gospel, and sustained us in the faith, set us to the tasks You reserved for us that we may be useful instruments in Your plan for mankind's deep needs; through Jesus Christ, our Lord, who with You and the Holy Spirit are one God with dominion over us forever.

Lesson I: Isaiah 49:1-6
The Gospel: John 1:29-41

Holy Spirit, charged with the presentation of the Son of the living God to the world, lead us continually to Your Scripture where Christ is presented for us, to the gathering where Christ has promised His presence, and to those who bring Him to us, that seeing Christ, we are renewed for our daily round of bearing witness to our Redeemer; through Jesus Christ, our Lord, who with You and the Father are one God with dominion over us forever.

===== B =====

Lesson II: 1 Corinthians 6:12-20

Heavenly Father, whose reign is over all created things, and who by Your justification in Christ have double dominion over us, Your highest creation and Your first love, instill in us the desire for a spirit of oneness with the Christ who by faith dwells in us; through Jesus Christ, our Lord, who with You and the Holy Spirit are one God with dominion over us forever.

Lesson I: 1 Samuel 3:1-10
The Gospel: John 1:43-51

Omniscient Lord, to whom all things are known and from whom nothing is hidden, accept our gratitude for accepting us where we are, and for loving us as we are, and hear our prayer to keep the memory of Your sacrifice and the hope of Your appearing in our minds; through Jesus Christ, our Lord, who with You and the Holy Spirit are one God with dominion over us forever.

C

Lesson II: 1 Corinthians 12:1-11

Holy Spirit, who calls us to faith and who dispenses the talents necessary to our community of faithful people, accept our gratitude for all Your gifts and talents to us and help each of us to share them with the community, that we may be helpful to it and that it in turn may be a blessing to each of us; through Jesus Christ, our Lord, who with You and the Father are one God with dominion over us forever.

Lesson I: Isaiah 62:1-5
The Gospel: John 2:1-11

Holy Spirit, in whose province lies the whole matter of sanctification, keep Christ the center of our lives, the core of our families, and the heart of our community, that in Christ our lives, our families, and our community may truly be set apart for God; through Jesus Christ, our Lord, who with You and the Father are one God with dominion over us forever.

Third Sunday After the Epiphany

=== A ===

Lesson II: 1 Corinthians 1:10-17

Holy and blessed Trinity, who though three Persons are one God, be in the midst of Your holy people that our unity in diversity may be the distinguishing mark of our common loyalty to You; through Jesus Christ, our Lord, who with the Father and the Holy Spirit are one God with dominion over us forever.

Lesson I: Isaiah 9:1b-4
("In the former time . . .") or Amos 3:1-8
The Gospel: Matthew 4:12-23

Holy Spirit, Builder of the Kingdom, so fill us with Yourself, Your power, and Your wisdom, that we may be able to fulfill the command of our Lord to speak the Gospel of the Kingdom to everyone; through Jesus Christ, our Lord, who with You and the Father are one God with dominion over us forever.

=== B ===

Lesson II: 1 Corinthians 7:29-31

Because You are active in applying the forgiveness of Jesus Christ to the sinful hearts of men, O Holy Spirit of God, love us into constant faithfulness to the kingdom of heaven, and woo the world to the Kingdom through us who are charged with proclaiming the Good News in our times; through Jesus Christ, our Lord, who with You and the Father are one God with dominion over us forever.

Lesson I: Jonah 3:1-5, 10
The Gospel: Mark 1:14-20

Great Judge, by whose wisdom the trumpeter appointed to

announce the end-time is stationed on the parapet, and to whom alone is known the hour for the signal to sound the end-time trumpet call, let the certainty of the uncertain time for the opening of heaven to all believers be for us yet another deterrent to evil deeds and yet another encouragement to maintain a proper perspective of our affairs in time; through Jesus Christ, our Lord, who with You and the Holy Spirit are one God with dominion over us forever.

C

Lesson II: 1 Corinthians 12:12-21, 26-27

Holy Spirit, Distributor of all good gifts, teach us to rejoice in the diversity of our gifts and to be willing to share ourselves with each other, that our community of Christ's people may be enriched and strengthened for greater service to the world in which we live; through Jesus Christ, our Lord, who with You and the Father are one God with dominion over us forever.

Lesson I: Isaiah 61:1-6

The Gospel: Luke 4:14-21

We pray You, merciful God, Father of our Lord Jesus Christ and our Father through Jesus Christ, fill the clamoring needs of our souls, the pangs of our bodies, and the yearning of our intellect with Christ, for we are whole and free only as He meets us in our bondage and our helplessness; through the same Jesus Christ, our Lord, who with You and the Holy Spirit are one God with dominion over us forever.

Fourth Sunday After the Epiphany

——— A ———

Lesson II: 1 Corinthians 1:26-31

Eternal God, who establishes the values to be prized by Your people, forgive us for adopting the world's standards, which betray us, and by the Spirit's power teach us to know the unsurpassable value You place on what seems to us so insignificant; through Jesus Christ, our Lord, who with You and the Holy Spirit are one God with dominion over us forever.

Lesson I: Micah 6:1-8
The Gospel: Matthew 5:1-12

Heavenly Father, for whom Jesus is spokesman, by the power of the Spirit in us change our hearts that we may be humble, merciful, pure in heart, pursuing righteousness and peace, as Jesus, Your Word, enjoined us once on a mountainside; through the same Jesus Christ, our Lord, who with You and the Holy Spirit are one Lord with dominion over us forever.

——— B ———

Lesson II: 1 Corinthians 8:1-13

Increase our faith and sharpen our judgment, Lord of the call and the commitment to Jesus Christ, that we be wise enough and strong enough, and considerate enough, to make right choices in the multitude of borderline decisions that confront us as Your disciples; through Jsus Christ, our Lord, who with You and the Father are one God with dominion over us forever.

34

Lesson I: Deuteronomy 18:15-20
The Gospel: Mark 1:21-28

Since Satan always recognizes You and quakes before You, Jesus Christ, keep us who are his natural prey faithful to You, and so dwell in us continually that when Satan comes tempting us to despair, Your presence in us bests him and keeps us safe; who with the Father and the Holy Spirit are one God with dominion over us forever.

C

Lesson II: 1 Corinthians 12:27—13:13

Heavenly Father, loving, and beloved of, Your only begotten Son, loving us in Your Son, let love, Yours and ours, be so in evidence in our community that people will take note of it and seek to know and glorify its Source; through Jesus Christ, our Lord, who with You and the Holy Spirit are one God with dominion over us forever.

Lesson I: Jeremiah 1:4-10
The Gospel: Luke 4:21-32

Holy Spirit, Caller, Gatherer, Enlightener, Keeper, confront us constantly with the deity of Jesus, sanctify us in the faith, and lead us to emulate Him in courageous assertion of our conviction, that Your work of building the Kingdom of Grace might be accomplished in the world; through Jesus Christ, our Lord, who with You and the Father are one God with dominion over us forever.

Fifth Sunday After The Epiphany

A

Lesson II: 1 Corinthians 2:1-5

Holy Spirit, who calls and sanctifies us by the Gospel proclamation alone, bless all who would evangelize the neighborhood with the wisdom that it is only in the proclamation of the Gospel that You have elected to call mankind to the saving faith; through Jesus Christ, our Lord, who with You and the Father are one God with dominion over us forever.

Lesson I: Isaiah 58:5-9a

The Gospel: Matthew 5:13-20

Heavenly Father, since it is true that our neighbor seeing our good works glorifies You, let our appreciation of Your love and forgiveness in Christ impel us to new determination to let our light shine in the darkness of the world for You; through Jesus Christ, our Lord, who with You and the Holy Spirit are one God with dominion over us forever.

B

Lesson II: 1 Corinthians 9:16-23

Holy Spirit, by whose power in the Word the borders of the Kingdom are extended, bid us follow the example of Paul, who for the sake of the Gospel was all things to all men in the Gospel freedom, that we might be fit channels for Your power and purpose in Kingdom building; through Jesus Christ, our Lord, who with You and the Father are one God with dominion over us forever.

Lesson I: Job 7:1-7
The Gospel: Mark 1:29-39

Divine Creator, from whose hand man came in glorious perfection, according to Your will for us be Physician or Comforter or Inspiration to us when there are laid on our bodies, minds, or souls burdens too difficult for us, that we might in them and beyond them see Your hand and heart; through Jesus Christ, our Lord, who with You and the Holy Spirit are one God with dominion over us forever.

C

Lesson II
1 Corinthians 14:12b-20 ("Since you are eager . . .")

Holy Spirit, Dispenser of gifts to the community of God's people, give us bountifully of the gifts that will edify the body of Christ in our place, that we may grow in faith, in spiritual things, and in holy living; through Jesus Christ, our Lord, who with You and the Father are one God with dominion over us forever.

Lesson I: Isaiah 6:1-8 (9-13)
The Gospel: Luke 5:1-11

Holy Spirit, Fisher of human beings on the God-side, so inspire us with the splendor of the King that we be faithful fishers of human beings on the people-side; through Jesus Christ, our Lord, who with You and the Father are one God with dominion over us forever.

Sixth Sunday After the Epiphany

A

Lesson II: 1 Corinthians 2:6-13

Holy Spirit, who dwells in the bosom of the Trinity and in our hearts, teach us to search the deep wisdom of God and, interpreting it for us, show us its application in our lives; through Jesus Christ, our Lord, who with You and the Father are one God with dominion over us forever.

Lesson I: Deuteronomy 30:15-20
The Gospel: Matthew 5:20-37

Holy Spirit, because God's justice apart from Christ terrifies us, do not let us ever revert to seeking our salvation in the demanding Law, but hold us steady in the Gospel, rejoicing in the freedom it guarantees us, through Jesus Christ, our Lord, who with You and the Father are one God with dominion over us forever.

Lesson II: 1 Corinthians 9:24-27

Mighty Spirit, from whom we receive such great and good gifts, grant us a clear vision of glory and patience and persistence to strive toward it in faith, lest by careless indifference we forfeit it forever; through Jesus Christ, our Lord, who with You and the Father are one God with dominion over us forever.

Lesson I: 2 Kings 5:1-14
The Gospel: Mark 1:40-45

Great Physician, whose word worked miracles and whose miracles drew people to You, nourish us today with the Word of life that makes and keeps us whole; who with the Father and the Holy Spirit are one God with dominion over us forever.

C

Lesson II: 1 Corinthians 15:12, 16-20

Heavenly Father, Lord of life and death, King of death and life, for
the atonement of Jesus Christ accomplished in obedience to You
and in love for us, and for the raising of Christ from the dead
accomplished in Your love for Him, daily increase in us the certain
hope of our immortality through a continuous strengthening of our
faith in our risen Lord; through the same Jesus Christ, our Lord,
who with You and the Holy Spirit are one God with dominion over
us forever.

Lesson I: Jeremiah 17:5-8
The Gospel: Luke 6:17-26

Holy Spirit, Sanctifier of our lives, guide us through a continuing
self-evaluation and bring us constantly to see and to embrace the
values of the Kingdom; through Jesus Christ, our Lord, who with
You and the Father are one God with dominion over us forever.

Seventh Sunday After the Epiphany

A

Lesson II: 1 Corinthians 3:10-11, 16-23

Holy Spirit, for whom our very bodies are temples in which You dwell, because You alone have brought us to our commitment to Jesus Christ through the Word, lead us always deeper into faith and trust in Christ; who with You and the Father are one God with dominion over us forever.

Lesson I: Leviticus 19:1-2, 17-18
The Gospel: Matthew 5:38-48

Heavenly Father, holy Judge, whose demands for righteousness exceed our ability to meet them, hear Christ, Your Son, our Advocate and Mediator, as He pleads our cause and hear us as we accept His substitution for us and plead His perfection as our own; through the same Jesus Christ, our Lord, who with You and the Holy Spirit are one God with dominion over us forever.

B

Lesson II: 2 Corinthians 1:18-22

Heavenly Father, ever faithful to Your Word, grant us such faithfulness that privately and publicly we affirm our commitment to You in every thought, word, and deed; through Jesus Christ, our Lord, who with You and the Holy Spirit are one God with dominion over us forever.

Lesson I: Isaiah 43:18-25
The Gospel: Mark 2:1-12

O blessed Trinity, Speaker of miracles and Doer of the Word, so let miracles and Word surround us that we be safe in every trial of our bodies, minds, or souls; in the name of Jesus Christ, our Lord, who with the Father and the Holy Spirit are one God with dominion over us forever.

C

Lesson II: 1 Corinthians 15:35-38a, 42-50

Heavenly Father, who has redeemed us through Jesus Christ by the power of the Holy Spirit, help us to live in this perishable body as people destined for the imperishable life of the hereafter; through Jesus Christ, our Lord, who with You and the Holy Spirit are one God with dominion over us forever.

Lesson I: Genesis 45:3-8a (" . . . but God.")
The Gospel: Luke 6:27-38

Blessed Jesus Christ, who sets the perimeters of Your love beyond all those who hated and crucified You, help us who would follow Your example in all things to bless as You blessed, to forgive as You forgave, and to love as You loved; who with the Father and the Holy Spirit are one God with dominion over us forever.

Eighth Sunday After the Epiphany

A

Lesson II: 1 Corinthians 4:1-13

Holy Spirit, Keeper of the divine mysteries and Steward of all Christian lives, encourage us who are servants of Christ in a faithful stewardship of the mysteries of God, and at the end let us receive the commendation of God; through Jesus Christ, our Lord, who with You and the Father are one God with dominion over us forever.

Lesson I: Isaiah 49:13-18

The Gospel: Matthew 6:24-34

Heavenly Father, whose evaluation of all spiritual and material things must finally be ours as well, hasten the day when we learn to make all judgments in the light of Christ and hold as dear to ourselves only that which is dear to You; through Jesus Christ our Lord, who with You and the Holy Spirit are one God with dominion over us forever.

B

Lesson II
2 Corinthians 3:1b-6 ("Do we need . . .")

Holy Spirit, who changes the hearts of people by the power of the Gospel of Jesus Christ, help us to make our lives good examples of people born anew into the freedom of the Kingdom, unburdened, unthreatened, and unfettered by the Law that would in the end defeat us; through the same Jesus Christ our Lord, who with You and the Father are one God with dominion over us forever.

Lesson I: Hosea 2:14-16 (17-18) 19-20

The Gospel: Mark 2:18-22

Lord of the old covenant shadows, whose incarnation fulfilled the ancient promises of Your coming, let us fast in freedom, remembering Your death and resurrection for us, lest fasting become an observation of the Law and a denial of the new freedom You have won for us; who with the Father and the Holy Spirit are one God with dominion over us forever.

C

Lesson II: 1 Corinthians 15:51-58

Gracious God, who has given us the victory over death through our Lord Jesus Christ, give us wisdom to value our immortal souls more highly than our perishable bodies and keep us in the holy Christian faith that dying we may live eternally; through Jesus Christ, our Lord, who with You and the Holy Spirit are one God with dominion over us forever.

Lesson I: Jeremiah 7:1-7 (8-15)
The Gospel: Luke 6:39-49

Holy Spirit, Sanctifier of our lives and Purifier of our hearts, so rule us that all our works done in the community of man are acceptable to God our Father and to Christ our Redeemer, who with You are one God with dominion over us forever.

The Transfiguration of Our Lord
Last Sunday After the Epiphany

A

Lesson II: 2 Peter 1:16-19 (20-21)

Holy Spirit, by whose power Your servants are moved to speak for God, and by whom the Scriptures are infused with power to convince us of the truths of God, help us that, moved by Your direction to make known the Word, we may proclaim it with faithfulness; through Jesus Christ, our Lord, who with You and the Father are one God with dominion over us forever.

Lesson I: Exodus 24:12, 15-18
The Gospel: Matthew 17:1-9

Heavenly Father, whose right to remain in the awesome mystery of Your being is unassailable, we are grateful for Your voice at Jesus' baptism and transfiguration, for You have thus authenticated His person and His mission before all the world; through the same Jesus Christ, our Lord, who with You and the Holy Spirit are one God with dominion over us forever.

B

Lesson II: 2 Corinthians 3:12—4:2

Spirit of the Lord, and Lord who is the Spirit, who in Christ makes clear the debilitating power of the old Law and in the same Christ makes clear the freeing power of the Gospel, give us wisdom to see the splendor of the great and wonderful things Christ has done for us; through the same Jesus Christ, our Lord, who with You and the Father are one God with dominion over us forever.

Lesson I
2 Kings 2:1—12a (" . . . saw him no more.")
The Gospel: Mark 9:2-9

As the Word recalls the Transfiguration event, Holy Spirit, Power in the Word, move us by our remembering of it to renewed faith, to deeper love, and to greater consecration until the appearing of the Son of Man, even Jesus Christ our Lord; who with the Father and the Holy Spirit are one God with dominion over us forever.

C

Lesson II: 2 Corinthians 4:3-6

Holy Spirit, in whose province and by whose unfathomable decision our election is made, secure us always in the faith which is in Christ lest we in our weakness change our allegiance to the gods of this world and lose our heritage; through Jesus Christ, our Lord, who with You and the Father are one God with dominion over us forever.

Lesson I: Deuteronomy 34:1-12
The Gospel: Luke 9:28-36

Lord Jesus Christ, Son of the living God, Savior of the world and our Savior, help us always to appreciate the wonder of Your person without losing sight of, or touch with, the world to which You have sent us; who with the Father and the Holy Spirit are one God with dominion over us forever.

Ash Wednesday

A, B, C

Lesson II
2 Corinthians 5:20b—6:2 ("We beseech you . . .")

Holy God, who by Jesus Christ reconciled justice and love, by the Spirit's power open our hearts to Your grace that we might know and enjoy the peace and freedom that our reconciliation with You makes available to us; through Jesus Christ, our Lord, who with You and the Holy Spirit are one God with dominion over us forever.

Or

Gracious and merciful God, whose justice calls for punishment for sin, we, by the Spirit's power, place our souls into the keeping of Christ, who came to our planet to reconcile us to You and to resolve the tension betweeen us forever; through Jesus Christ, our Lord, who with You and the Holy Spirit are one God with dominion over us forever.

Or

Be with us, gracious Father, who gave Your only begotten Son to die for us, as we behold again Him who was made to be sin for us in His suffering and death and remember with gratitude that but for Your grace in Him we should have so been judged and condemned; through Jesus Christ, our Lord, who with You and the Holy Spirit are one God with dominion over us forever.

Lesson I: Joel 2:12-19
The Gospel: Matthew 6:1-6, 16-21

Heavenly Father, God of the right hand, Lord of the private prayer place, grant us grace to fast, to pray, and to do charity in secret, for we would not want our neighbor to confuse our deeds with our faith in our Redeemer; through the same Jesus Christ, our Lord, who with You and the Holy Spirit are one God with dominion over us forever.

Or

Eternal Judge, whose demand for works is exceeded by the faith requirement, forgive us the satisfaction we take in our works and piety and lead us to deeper trust in Christ, our Savior, lest we be numbered with the goats in the final judgment; through Jesus Christ, our Lord, who with You and the Holy Spirit are one God with dominion over us forever.

Or

Dear Father in heaven, who having created us knows well our frailties, purify our motives for all our works, that they proceed from faith in Christ, our Redeemer, and be done because we love You above all else; through Jesus Christ, our Lord, who with You and the Holy Spirit are one God with dominion over us forever.

First Sunday in Lent

Lesson II: Romans 5:12 (13-16) 17-19

Holy Spirit, called in by Christ, our Lord, to guide us in the faith, lead us past Adam, the Law, and Moses, which brings us only despair, to the Christ and His holy Gospel with forgiveness and righteousness; through Jesus Christ, our Lord, who with You and the Father are one God with dominion over us forever.

Lesson I: Genesis 2:7-9, 15-17; 3:1-7
The Gospel: Matthew 4:1-11

Holy Spirit, as You led Jesus, the Christ, into the wilderness to be tempted by the Evil One, lead us out of all temptations that come to us by Satan, the world, and our flesh, that by Your power and leading we may emerge from our wilderness as victorious as our Savior left His; through Jesus Christ, our Lord, who with You and the Father are one God with dominion over us forever.

Lesson II: Romans 8:31-39

God, who is Love, enable us by faith to pierce all adversity to see beyond and through it Your constant love for us in Christ Jesus, that in all that hurts or deceives us we are sustained and strengthened through Jesus Christ, our Friend and Redeemer; through the same Jesus Christ, our Lord, who with You and the Holy Spirit are one God with dominion over us forever.

Lesson I: Genesis 22:1-18
The Gospel: Mark 1:12-15

Holy Spirit, Imparter of faith, Donor of trust, who sent Christ to the fearful wilderness experience, be with us in our times of temptation so that if the temptation be of God we are purified and strengthened by it, or if it be of Satan we stay faithful to our Christ in the midst of it; through the same Jesus Christ, our Lord, who with You and the Father are one God with dominion over us forever.

C

Lesson II
Romans 10:8b-13 ("The word is near . . .")

Heavenly Father, Creator of all, Judge of all, by the power of the Spirit open our hearts to Christ that we may make an honest confession of Him with our lips and be saved in the hour of judgment; through Jesus Christ, our Lord, who with You and the Holy Spirit are one God with dominion over us forever.

Lesson I: Deuteronomy 26:5-10
The Gospel: Luke 4:1-13

Heavenly Father, protect us who have made our commitment to Christ from the bombarding temptations of Satan, for we would neither dishonor You nor forfeit our share in Your kingdom; through Jesus Christ, our Lord, who with You and the Holy Spirit are one God with dominion over us forever.

Second Sunday in Lent

─── A ───

Lesson II: Romans 4:1-5, 13-17

Heavenly Father, who demands an impossible perfection and then in Jesus Christ confers righteousness upon the faithful, let Christ's righteousness in us compel us to such life and living that the world will take note and offer You praise and honor; through Jesus Christ, our Lord, who with You and the Holy Spirit are one God with dominion over us forever.

Lesson I: Genesis 12:1-8
The Gospel: John 4:5-26 (27-30, 39-42)

Blessed Jesus, as once You shattered the limitations of faith so long controlled by the Law, shatter all contemporary illusions that restrain the Gospel and its explosive power for the community of the faithful and the family of man; who with the Father and the Holy Spirit are one God with dominion over us forever.

─── B ───

Lesson II: Romans 5:1-11

We stagger, almighty God, whose justice demands death for sin— we stagger at the height and depth of Your love for us sinners, for by it we have been snatched from judgment and death for freedom and for life in the reconciliation effected by Jesus Christ; through the same Jesus Christ, our Lord, who with You and the Holy Spirit are one God with dominion over us forever.

Lesson I: Genesis 28:10-17 (18-22)
The Gospel: Mark 8:31-38

Lord Jesus Christ, whose devotion to the Father and dedication to us surpass our comprehension, let us hold You as example that we be strong in temptation and zealous for all good works and thus call all the world to glorify Your Father and ours; who with the Father and the Holy Spirit are one God with dominion over us forever.

C

Lesson II: Philippians 3:17—4:1

Holy Spirit, Elector to grace, Filler of hearts, Producer of the righteous life, guarantee our election, fill us with faith and pour out of our lives, that everyone whom we touch in our daily round may glorify our Father and our Lord Jesus Christ, whose eternal city we represent in mission here and now; through Jesus Christ, our Lord, who with You and the Father are one God with dominion over us forever.

Lesson I: Jeremiah 26:8-15
The Gospel: Luke 13:31-35

Gracious and terrible God, whose justice metes out the death wage for sin and whose grace is freely offered to all in Jesus, the Christ, translate our grateful hearts into grace-filled lives, that all humanity learn to know of Your love and in the end many share heaven with Christ and all the saints; through the same Jesus Christ, our Lord, who with You and the Holy Spirit are one God with dominion over us forever.

Third Sunday in Lent

A

Lesson II: Ephesians 5:8-14

Holy Spirit, who has called us out of spiritual darkness to the light of Christ, grant us the will and the wisdom to live by the light of Christ, beacons indeed for the Father in this world; through Jesus Christ, our Lord, who with You and the Father are one God with dominion over us forever.

Lesson I: Isaiah 42:14-21
The Gospel
John 9:1-41 (long) or John 9:13-17, 34-39 (short)

Beloved Jesus, who gave sight to the blind and who opens the windows of the soul, enable us, who by grace are sighted people, to see our fellow-redeemed with Your compassion and to see the promised mansions with Your certainty; who with the Father and the Holy Spirit are one God with dominion over us forever.

B

Lesson II: 1 Corinthians 1:22-25

Omniscient and all-sufficient God, before whom we are but creatures, lead us past the barriers in our minds and souls that hinder our commitment to Your Christ, our Redeemer, lest, knowing Him without faith, we lose the forgiveness He won for us and the inheritance in glory He opened to us by His cross; through Jesus Christ, our Lord, who with You and the Holy Spirit are one God with dominion over us forever.

Lesson I: Exodus 20:1-17
The Gospel: John 2:13-22

Holy Spirit, in whose care is our faith and life, keep Your church and us aware that in matters of the Kingdom mind and heart need to be involved before the outward form of expression, for if our worship be void of mind and heart, it is but hollow bleating and cooing; through Jesus Christ, our Lord, who with You and the Father are one God with dominion over us forever.

C

Lesson II: 1 Corinthians 10:1-13

Gracious Lord, who stands beside us on the battlefields of life, keep us conscious of Your faithful presence on the plain, of Your intervention in our continuous spiritual struggles, and of Your victory over all the sins which so often beset us, that we may by Your love and nearness be conquerors in every trial and victors over every evil; who with the Father and the Holy Spirit are one God with dominion over us forever.

Lesson I
Exodus 3:1-8b (" . . . milk and honey."), 10-15
The Gospel: Luke 13:1-9

Holy Father, whose preservation saves creation from annihilation and whose patience with sinful people is a mark of Your love for them, deliver us in the day of our death, keeping us in the saving faith generated by the Cross and guaranteed by the Holy Spirit; through Jesus Christ, our Lord, who with You and the Holy Spirit are one God with dominion over us forever.

Fourth Sunday in Lent

A

Lesson II: Romans 8:1-10

Holy Trinity, who has made our bodies Your dwelling place, since we cannot trust our reason or the Law which lead to death, be our guide to glory; through Jesus Christ, our Lord, who with the Father and the Holy Spirit are one God with dominion over us forever.

Lesson I: Hosea 5:15—6:2
The Gospel: Matthew 20:17-28

Blessed Jesus, who went up to Jerusalem to be delivered to our death, let Your example of great love and humble service guide us in our relations with our fellowmen on our journey to the mansions for which You have redeemed us; through Jesus Christ, our Lord, who with the Father and the Holy Spirit are one God with dominion over us forever.

B

Lesson II: Ephesians 2:4-10

God of glory, God of mercy, who by the Spirit and the Word has made us new creatures in Christ Jesus, impell us by that same Spirit and Word to live lives equal to Your blessing, that there be no doubt whose workmanship we are; through Jesus Christ, our Lord, who with You and the Holy Spirit are one God with dominion over us forever.

Lesson I: Numbers 21:4-9
The Gospel: John 3:14-21

God of infinite love, whose we are by the death of Christ, Your Son, let the vision and import of the cross fill us with such love that we worship and adore You and minister to friend and enemy alike because of it; through Jesus Christ, our Lord, who with You and the Holy Spirit are one God with dominion over us forever.

C

Lesson II
1 Corinthians 1:18-31 or 1 Corinthians 1:18, 22-25

Holy God, whose attributes are omniscience and omnipotence, help us to see and know the wisdom and power of the cross of Christ for our peace and hope in this world where human wisdom and power are too often mistaken for life's ultimate good; through Jesus Christ, our Lord, who with You and the Holy Spirit are one God with dominion over us forever.

Lesson I: Isaiah 12:1-6
The Gospel: Luke 15:1-3, 11-32

Heavenly Father, who desires to rule over us and who would live in us, open our hearts to the Holy Spirit's prompting, that the distance our old Adam would maintain between us may be bridged by the reconciliation Your love and grace has brought about through our Savior, Jesus Christ; through the same Jesus Christ, our Lord, who with You and the Holy Spirit are one God with dominion over us forever.

Fifth Sunday in Lent

A

Lesson II: Romans 8:11-19

Holy Spirit, Sanctifier of our lives, dwell in us and bear constant witness to us of our relationship with the Father that we avoid what is displeasing to Him who gave us His Son to death that we might have eternal life; through Jesus Christ, our Lord, who with You and the Father are one God with dominion over us forever.

Lesson I: Ezekiel 37:1-3 (4-10) 11-14
The Gospel
John 11:1-53 (long); John 11:47-53 (short)

Blessed Lord Jesus Christ, who is the Resurrection and the Life, may our gratitude for the glory life which Your death assures us find expression in our lives in prayer and service until the angel trumpets summon us to come to You; who with the Father and the Holy Spirit are one God with dominion over us forever.

B

Lesson II: Hebrews 5:7-9

Heavenly Father, whose Son demonstrated and became the Way of right relationship with You, open us, who travel the path of faith and reconciliation, to the sanctifying of the Spirit that we walk as Your disciples and as humble examples to the world; through Jesus Christ, our Lord, who with You and the Holy Spirit are one God with dominion over us forever.

Lesson I: Jeremiah 31:31-34
The Gospel: John 12:20-33

Gracious Judge, in whose courts the judgment of the world takes place, for the visible demonstration of Your mercy toward us in the death of Your Son and our Savior on Execution Hill, we offer grateful hearts for our own salvation and new life and for the salvation of the whole world; through Jesus Christ, our Lord, who with You and the Holy Spirit are one God with dominion over us forever.

C

Lesson II: Philippians 3:8-14

Holy Spirit of the divine Godhead, who convinces us by the Word of the preeminence of Christ, guide us to the Word, lead us in the Word, keep us under the Word, that Christ may have sole dominion over us and that we strive to be His imitators; through the same Jesus Christ, our Lord, who with You and the Father are one God with dominion over us forever.

Lesson I: Isaiah 43:16-21

The Gospel: Luke 20:9-19

Heavenly Father, Lord of the vineyard, God of Your people, bend our hearts and shape our lives that Christ always be welcome among us lest we who are Your people, denying and rejecting the Cornerstone, be ourselves pruned from the Vine and be cast upon the fire; through Jesus Christ, our Lord, who with You and the Holy Spirit are one God with dominion over us forever.

Sunday of the Passion

Palm Sunday

A

Lesson II: Philippians 2:5-11

Holy God, who loved rebellious mankind so deeply as to give Your Son for us, we are so overwhelmed by the burden of His descent from glory to awesome isolation and so equally overwhelmed by the splendor of His return to exaltation that we, so loved, are without words to thank and praise You; in the name of Jesus Christ, our Lord, who with You and the Holy Spirit are one God with dominion over us forever.

Or

Second Adam, Jesus Christ, who made Yourself of no reputation to serve us, teach us to know that we are creatures, purchased with Your life to be sons and daughters, that we might serve You even as we expend ourselves for the family of man; who with the Father and the Holy Spirit are one God with dominion over us forever.

Or

Holy Spirit, by whose persuasion we are brought to new life in Christ, let the mind of Christ be in each of us that as redeemed creatures we keep our proper place in relation to our heavenly Father and in relation to our fellow human beings; through Jesus Christ, our Lord, who with You and the Father are one God with dominion over us forever.

Or

Heavenly Father, whose solution to the problem of our sins necessitated the sacrifice of Your Son on the cross, teach us, who bow our knees at the name of Jesus, obedience like to His in the ordering of our lives, that they may be a living testimonial to our gratitude to both of You; through Jesus Christ, our Lord, who with You and the Holy Spirit are one God with dominion over us forever.

Lesson I
Isaiah 50:4-9a (" . . . declare me guilty?")
The Gospel
Matthew 26:1—27:66 (long) Matthew 27:11-54 (short)

Blessed Jesus, who for our sins suffered the terror of the Father's wrath and for our eternities endured the desolation of the Father's judgment, accept our gratitude and praise: Hosanna! Blessed be the Son of God who has redeemed us; Hosanna in the highest! who with the Father and the Holy Spirit are one God with dominion over us forever.

B

Lesson II: Philippians 2:5-11

See A

Lesson I: Zechariah 9:9-10
The Gospel
Mark 14:1—15:47 (long); Mark 15:1-39 (short)

Hosanna to You, redeeming Lord, whose procession of triumph came to its climax on the hill of Calvary, for You, who are truly the Son of God, held steady to Your course until in dying You accomplished Your holy purpose of the world's redemption: Hosanna to the Son of the living God! who with the Father and the Holy Spirit alone are worthy of our praise and adoration, one God with dominion over us forever.

59

C

Lesson II: Philippians 2:5-11

See A

Lesson I: Deuteronomy 32:36-39
The Gospel
Luke 22:1—23:56 (long); Luke 23:1-49 (short)

Heavenly Father, whose will alone motivated Jesus, the Christ, to the atonement, restrain us from praising Jesus and demeaning Christ by mistaking the purpose of His mighty works, but let us rather praise Christ who is Jesus, God made man to redeem us, whose mighty works call us to the cross; through the same Jesus Christ, our Lord, who with You and the Holy Spirit are one God with dominion over us forever.

Maundy Thursday

A

Lesson II: 1 Corinthians 11:17-32 (long)
1 Corinthians 11:23-26 (short)

Beloved Lord Jesus Christ, through whom on the night of the betrayal the Father gave to His church His new covenant, let us celebrate the blessed Sacrament, seal of the Father's covenant, remembering Your death in our stead, sure of Your presence with us even now, and full of hope and expectation of Your imminent return in splendor; who with the Father and the Holy Spirit are one God with dominion over us forever.

Lesson I: Exodus 12:1-14
The Gospel: John 13:1-17, 34

Beloved Jesus, who on the night of your betrayal knelt to wash the feet of Your disciples, help us to be such honest and willing servants that we love all people in word and deed, and in our hearts as well; who with the Father and the Holy Spirit are one God with dominion over us forever.

B

Lesson II: 1 Corinthians 10:16-17 (18-21)

Holy Spirit, through whom purpose and power are given to the Word and Sacrament, bless us this night/day as we participate in the cup of blessing and the breaking of bread with heightened appreciation of our blessed Lord who redeemed us and of each other who are the redeemed, that we may have here a haven from the sinful world in which we must live; through Jesus Christ, our Lord, who with the Father and the Holy Spirit are one God with dominion over us forever.

Lesson I: Exodus 24:3-11
The Gospel: Mark 14:12-26

Blessed Son of God, Jesus Christ, our Lord, who in a borrowed room set the guarantee of your perpetual love with Your body and blood given and shed for us, we confess our utter unworthiness for such great concern, but we receive it with thanksgiving for without it we perish; who with the Father and the Holy Spirit are one God with dominion over us forever.

C

Lesson II: Hebrews 10:15-39

Holy God, most worthy and eternal Judge, forgive us our lack of faith in, and our faithlessness to, Christ and, by the indwelling Spirit, guide our faith and lives in Your way of obedience born of an appreciation of Your Christ-giving love for us; through the same Jesus Christ, our Lord, who with You and the Holy Spirit are one God with dominion over us forever.

Lesson I: Jeremiah 31:31-34
The Gospel: Luke 22:7-20

Holy God, who deals with us in steadfast love, for the abrogation of the demanding Old Covenant at the cost of the holy precious blood of Your Christ and for the establishment of the New Covenant with us, signed and sealed in Christ's body and blood, we thank and praise You; through Jesus Christ, our Lord, who with You and the Holy Spirit are one God with dominion over us forever.

Good Friday

A, B, C

Lesson II: Hebrews 4:14-16; 5:7-9

Lord Jesus, appointed High Priest after the order of Melchizedek by the Father, since Your obedience to Him even to death for our sins has worked our redemption, let the same elicit continued praise and thanksgiving and become our reason for obedience to the Father's holy will; who with the Father and the Holy Spirit are one God with dominion over us forever.

Or

Jesus, Son of God, appointed by the Father to be our High Priest, we say our profoundest gratitude to You, for in obedience to Your Father You offered prayers and supplication, You suffered and died, that we through obedience to You might obtain eternal salvation; who with the Father and the Holy Spirit are one God with dominion over us forever.

Lesson I: Isaiah 52:13—53:12 or Hosea 6:1-6
The Gospel
John 18:1—19:42 (long); John 19:17-30 (short)

Beloved Jesus, who is King over all people and who ruled from the cross in majesty and glory, we weep for sinful humanity and pray with You that all people look to Your cross for forgiveness and Your throne in hope; who with the Father and the Holy Spirit are one God with dominion over us forever.

Or

Holy God, who is greatly displeased by our sins and who has spoken judgment against us, since we can scarcely imagine or comprehend

63

the awesomeness of Your wrath or the severity of our judgment without deep fear and trembling, we plead our Jesus who interposed Himself between You and us, as our Savior from Your judgment and our way back to Your love-filled heart; hear us for Jesus' sake, who with You and the Holy Spirit are one God with dominion over us forever.

The Resurrection of Our Lord

Easter Day

A

Lesson II: Colossians 3:1-4

O Lord Jesus Christ, who, the redemption of the world accomplished, yielded Your life, and who, after burial in the cold grave, was raised by the glory of the Father, fill our trembling hearts with faith and confidence now and hold us in joyous expectation until You greet us in glory; who with the Father and the Holy Spirit are one God with dominion over us forever.

Lesson I: Acts 10:34-43
The Gospel
John 20:1-9 (10-18) or Matthew 28:1-10

Hallelujah! Living and reigning Lord, upon whom the Father laid the sins of us all, because in obedience to Your Father's will and in love for us You forfeited Your life, You sit now at His direction in regal splendor on His right hand; we adore You and will honor You with praise and righteous living; Hallelujah! O Jesus Christ, our Lord, who with the Father and the Holy Spirit are one God with dominion over us forever.

B

Lesson II: 1 Corinthians 15:19-28

Holy Spirit, keep us faithful to the Christ, that dying we may come to glory, and that in glory we may be present at the majestic moment when the Son presents the Kingdom of Grace to His Father amid the mighty choruses of all the heavenly hosts; through Jesus Christ, our Lord, who with You and the Father are one God with dominion over us forever.

Lesson I: Isaiah 25:6-9
The Gospel: Mark 16:1-8

Hallelujah! Eternal Father, whose justice has been satisfied by the death of Jesus Christ and whose acceptance of His death is heralded by His rising on the third day, we praise You for our forgiveness and thank You for our blessed hope in Jesus Christ: Hallelujah; through Jesus Christ, our Lord, who with You and the Holy Spirit are one God with dominion over us forever.

Or John 20:1-9 (10-18)

Hallelujah! You rose from the dead! You live! You reign, Lord over us, Jesus, the Christ of God! Hallelujah! Come to us! Touch us! Love us! Guide us! Lead us! Take us! In Your death we died with You! In Your resurrection we rise with You! In glory we shall reign with You! Hallelujah! Hallelujah! who with the Father and the Holy Spirit are one God with dominion over us forever.

C

Lesson II: 1 Corinthians 15:1-11

Holy Spirit, with power to create faith without sight, help us to see through the eyes of faith, lest failing to see, we lose the victory of Christ's resurrection; through the same Jesus Christ, our Lord, who with You and the Father are one God with dominion over us forever.

Lesson I: Exodus 15:1-11 or Psalm 118:14-24
The Gospel: Luke 24:1-11

Hallelujah! Eternal Father, who raised Your Son from the grave, we praise and glorify You, for in the resurrection of Christ we have been freed from the terror of Your judgment and the tyranny of eternal death. Hallelujah! through Jesus Christ, our Lord, who with You and the Holy Spirit are one God with dominion over us forever.

Or John 20:1-9 (10-18).

See Gospel for Series B.

Second Sunday of Easter

A

Lesson II: 1 Peter 1:3-9

Beloved Jesus, Christ of God, Redeemer of our souls and Assurance of our salvation, hear our fumbling attempts to put our praise and gratitude into words and know our unutterable and exalted joy that in faith we hold You and that You hold us now and forever; who with the Father and the Holy Spirit are one God with dominion over us forever.

Lesson I: Acts 2:14a
(" . . . and addressed them:"), 22-32
The Gospel: John 20:19-31

Holy Spirit, Guardian and Dispenser of the holy faith, help us always to see our fellow human beings through the eyes of the crucified and risen Christ, for we will most certainly fail in our responsibility to them if we do not; through Jesus Christ, our Lord, who with You and the heavenly Father are one God with dominion over us forever.

B

Lesson II: 1 John 5:1-6

Lord Jesus Christ, as You came in love to love us to the death, grant us, being so loved, to love each other in response, that the mark of God's community be upon us who call ourselves a Christian congregation; who with the Father and the Holy Spirit are one God with dominion over us forever.

Lesson I: Acts 3:13-15, 17-26
The Gospel: John 20:19-31

Lord Jesus, risen Lord, whose love suffers long and is kind, as You were once patient with Thomas, the doubter, be patient with us and show us the nailholes again lest our humanness get in the way of our faith; who with the Father and the Holy Spirit are one God with dominion over us forever. ·

C

Lesson II: Revelation 1:4-18

King of kings, and Lord of lords, to whom are given the keys of heaven and hell and the lordship of all history by the will of the Father, keep us who are called by the Gospel—and by the Gospel call bring many people under the benevolence and the security of Your dominion, that they may know and serve You as Lord; who with the Father and the Holy Spirit are one God with dominion over us forever.

Lesson I: Acts 5:12, 17-32
The Gospel: John 20:19-31

Holy Lord God, whose desire is that the whole world confess Christ, help us to understand that seeing Christ in the Word and Sacraments ordains us to the royal priesthood and sets us in mission to the world with the Word and Sacraments that all people may see Christ, the Savior; through the same Jesus Christ, our Lord, who with You and the Holy Spirit are one God with dominion over us forever.

Third Sunday of Easter

Lesson II: 1 Peter 1:17-21

Beloved Christ, who lived, died and rose again for our justification, guide us in all our thoughts and deeds that our behavior during this time of exile honors You and glorifies the Father; who with the Father and the Holy Spirit are one God with dominion over us forever.

Lesson I: Acts 2:14a, 36-47
The Gospel: Luke 24:13-35

Holy Spirit, whose assignment within the Godhead is the building of the Kingdom of Grace, keep the vision of the redeeming and reigning Christ before us in all its radiance, for we fear living in the shadows and so losing our Kingdom citizenship; through Jesus Christ, our Lord, who with You and the Father are one God with dominion over us forever.

Lesson II: 1 John 1:1—2:2

Lord Jesus Christ, Champion and Advocate of sinners at the tribunal of the Father, in spite of our disparity draw us ever deeper into the fellowship of light and love, that we may the more appreciate Your gracious presence among us and all that You do to make Your peace work in our midst; who with the Father and the Holy Spirit are one God with dominion over us forever.

Lesson I: Acts 4:8-12
The Gospel: John 24:36-49

God, Father of the human family, whose love for us all is so forcibly visible on Calvary, excite us in our redemption through Christ that we witness the news to the multitudes within the human family who still call Adam father and stand in danger of the Judgment; through Jesus Christ, our Lord, who with You and the Holy Spirit are one God with dominion over us forever.

C

Lesson II: Revelation 5:11-14

Christ, sacrificial Lamb slain for us, we offer You blessing and honor and glory and might with our hearts and lips, and we lay our heads and hands before You for service in Your kingdom; who with the Father and the Holy Spirit are one God with dominion over us forever.

Lesson I: Acts 9:1-20
The Gospel: John 21:1-14

Holy Spirit, to whom the Trinitarian councils assigned the heralding of the reconciliation and the resurrection of Christ, since You have elected us by grace to be Your witnesses to Christ, supply us with courage to speak and live Christ, and add power to our proclamation in order that the Kingdom be extended by those whom You add to it, to the honor and glory of our risen and reigning Christ; who with You and the Father are one God with dominion over us forever.

Fourth Sunday of Easter

A

Lesson II: 1 Peter 2:19-25 *

Gentle Shepherd, strong Guardian of our souls, since we would be hopelessly lost in this world without Your strong hand to protect us and Your tender love to care for us, stay with us, for without You we are altogether defenseless against the enemies of our souls; who with the Father and the Holy Spirit are one God with dominion over us forever.

Lesson I: Acts 6:1-9, 7:2a, 51-60
The Gospel: John 10:1-10 *

Gracious Jesus Christ, good Shepherd of the Father's flock and strong Door of His fold, we thank You for the constancy of Your shepherding, for without You we would have no security in the world and no guide to the Father's mansions; who with the Father and the Holy Spirit are one God with dominion over us forever.

B

Lesson II: 1 John 3:1-2 *

Abba, Father, and Father of our Lord Jesus Christ, we live in excited anticipation of seeing You face to face and discovering Your promised newness of life in eternity, thus receiving Your final gift of life to us; through Jesus Christ, our Lord, who with You and the Holy Spirit are one God with dominion over us forever.

Lesson I: Acts 4:23-33
The Gospel: John 10:11-18 *

Gracious Lord, Shepherd of our lives and Guardian of our souls, who has set us all to shepherding each other, give us time, determination, and opportunity to share with others the kind of love and care that You constantly give to us; who with the Father and the Holy Spirit are one God with dominion over us forever.

C

Lesson II: Revelation 7:9-17 *

Gentle Jesus, mighty Shepherd, let us here sing glory songs with all redeemed sinners and there before Your throne with all the saints; who with the Father and the Holy Spirit are one God with dominion over us forever.

Lesson I
Acts 13:15-16a (" . . . his hands said:"), 26-33
The Gospel: John 10:22-30 *

Mighty Jesus, gentle Shepherd, who has called us to follow You, lead us through the weal and woe of this world to the splendor of the world to come; who with the Father and the Holy Spirit are one God with dominion over us forever.

---

* All Good Shepherd collects are interchangeable.

Fifth Sunday of Easter

A

Lesson II: 1 Peter 2:4-10

Holy Spirit, who in the waters of our baptism ordained us to priesthood, equip us by the Word and faith to proclaim the kingdom of God, that all who have rejected the Headstone of the Corner, be given a second opportunity to become living and lively stones in the house of God; through Jesus Christ, our Lord, who with You and the Father are one God with dominion over us forever.

Lesson I: Acts 17:1-15

The Gospel: John 14:1-12

Blessed Jesus, who opened the gate of Paradise to give us access to the Father's heart, lead us to follow Your example of devotion at the open doors until we are called to come through them to sing His high praise with all the saints and angels on the other side; who with the Father and the Holy Spirit are one God with dominion over us forever.

B

Lesson II: 1 John 3:18-24

Jesus, Lover of our souls, whose commands call us to obedience to Your will, keep us reminded of Your incomparable love for us that we in faith and obedience love each other and all others to Your honor and praise; who with the Father and the Holy Spirit are one God with dominion over us forever.

Lesson I: Acts 8:26-40

The Gospel: John 15:1-8

Eternal Father, Dresser of the Vine and branches, who supplies life through Your Son, the Vine, that we, the branches, might bear fruit, make our lives rich with fruit for the harvest by maintaining in us a right relationship with Christ and through careful pruning of the Old Adam in us; through Jesus Christ, our Lord, who with You and the Holy Spirit are one God with dominion over us forever.

C

Lesson II: Revelation 21:1-5

Mighty God, enthroned in glory, Ruler of all good and evil, hasten the day when evil is defeated and all things are made new, that only praise and thanksgiving, unmixed with cursing and swearing, be tendered to You by all Your people; through Jesus Christ, our Lord, who with You and the Holy Spirit are one God with dominion over us forever.

Lesson I: Acts 13:44-52

The Gospel: John 13:31-35

Heavenly Father, whose love and concern for us are perfectly demonstrated in Jesus Christ, our Redeemer, let the power and wonder of Your love so fill us that we cannot but love our fellow-redeemed, lovable and unlovable alike, for their sake and for Yours; through Jesus Christ, our Lord, who with You and the Holy Spirit are one God with dominion over us forever.

Sixth Sunday of Easter

A

Lesson II: 1 Peter 3:15-22 ("In your hearts . . .")

Holy Spirit, who calls and gathers a people for God through the revelation of the mystery of Jesus Christ by those who know and believe it, give all who are committed to Christ the ability to expresss their relationship with Him that they may be able to make a good witness to anyone who questions their motive for doing good; through Jesus Christ, our Lord, who with You and the Father are one God with dominion over us forever.

Lesson I: Acts 17:22-31
The Gospel: John 14:15-21

Gracious Christ, who with Your suffering and death redeemed the world and who promised to dwell in Your faithful people on their appointed mission, accept our gratitude for our redemption from the world and keep us aware of the presence of the Godhead in us as we go back to proclaim its redemption to it; who with the Father and the Holy Spirit are one God with dominion over us forever.

B

Lesson II: 1 John 4:1-11

God, Source of love, whose love is manifested by the crucified and risen Jesus, hold us in Your love so strongly that we cannot but love one another as You love us; through Jesus Christ, our Lord, who with You and the Holy Spirit are one God with dominion over us forever.

Lesson I: Acts 11:19-30
The Gospel: John 15:9-17

Heavenly Father, through whose heart love flows freely to the

76

heart of Jesus, whose great heart in turn embraces all people, let us love in our turn and so make our humble contribution to the peace and unity You desire for all mankind; through Jesus Christ, our Lord, who with You and the Holy Spirit are one God with dominion over us forever.

C

Lesson II: Revelation 21:10-14, 22-23

Holy Spirit, who opened the vision of the consummation of the Kingdom to Your ancient seer, increase our faith that we too might see the splendor of God and the glory of the Lamb, the light of the holy city, drawing us through life in time to life eternal; through Jesus Christ, our Lord, who with You and the Father are one God with dominion over us forever.

Lesson I: Acts 14:8-18

The Gospel: John 14:23-29

Holy Spirit, who through Word and Sacrament calls and keeps us in the holy faith, help us to requite the Father's love for us, for to do less would be a denial of His Word and promises to us and invite upon us His displeasure and wrath; through Jesus Christ, our Lord, who with You and the Father are one God with dominion over us forever.

The Ascension of Our Lord

A, B, C

Lesson II: Ephesians 1:16-23

Transcendent Christ, by whose authority and power all created things exist, and under whose dominion the holy church has its being, keep us, Your people, in safety in the world and bless us whom You call beloved with all spiritual blessings; who with the Father and the Holy Spirit are one God with dominion over us forever.

Or

Heavenly Father, Lord of Glory, who showers us with so many and such great gifts in Christ, our Lord, we are aware that we in no way merit them, and we are grateful beyond words for them; through Jesus Christ, our Lord, who with You and the Holy Spirit are one God with dominion over us forever.

Or

By the vision of Your throne in heavenly places, from whence You have rule and authority, power and dominion over every name and creature and thing, draw Your church to You, Lord Jesus Christ, who was raised from the dead having freed us from the Father's wrath and judgment, and who, at the Father's invitation, has been seated at His right hand in glory; who now with the Father and the Holy Spirit are one God with dominion over us forever.

Lesson I: Acts 1:1-11
The Gospel: Luke 24:44-53

High and exalted Christ, sitting at the right hand of the Father in power and great glory, we constantly covet Your watchfulness for it is only as You bless our lives that life has meaning, purpose, and destination; who with the Father and the Holy Spirit are one God with dominion over us forever.

Or

Jesus Christ, our Lord, acclaimed by men and angels, we thank and praise You that we who are commissioned to live and work wherever there are people are always surrounded by the mountains of Your presence and power which sustain and strengthen us; who with the Father and the Holy Spirit are one God with dominion over us forever.

Or

Lord Jesus, Lord of glory, who redeemed us to God by Your death and resurrection, and who even now sits in power at God's right hand, receive our faltering earthly praise and honor, and hasten the day when the whole church on earth enters the Kingdom of Glory to sing the songs of heaven with the great retinue of cherubim and angels, seraphim and saints gathered around Your throne; who with the Father and the Holy Spirit are one God with dominion over us forever.

Seventh Sunday of Easter

========== A ==========

Lesson II: 1 Peter 4:12-17; 5:6-11

Holy God, at once our Creator, Redeemer, and Sanctifier, hold martyrdom far from us, but should it be required of us, keep our commitment to You so constant that it is only the doorway to the mansions for us; through Jesus Christ, our Lord, who with the Father and the Holy Spirit is one God with dominion over us forever.

Lesson I: Acts 1:(1-7) 8-14
The Gospel: John 17:1-11

Blessed Holy Spirit, Guardian of the holy catholic church, the communion of saints, forgive us our division of the community of Christ, for while it is in our search for truth that division becomes possible, it is in our pride that it becomes reality, but let us rather follow Your example of forgiveness, love, and ministry for the well-being of the whole communion of saints; through Jesus Christ, our Lord, who with You and the Father are one God with dominion over us forever.

========== B ==========

Lesson II: 1 John 4:13-21

Holy Spirit, by whose power alone faith and sanctification are generated and sustained, move us who are in the church from faith to love to unity that the Christian community be the example of love in action in the world; for the sake of Jesus Christ, our Lord, who with You and the Father are one God with dominion over us forever.

Lesson I: Acts 1:15-26
The Gospel: John 17:11b-19

Heavenly Father, who heard the High Priestly intercession of
Christ the night in which He was betrayed, continually give
answer to His petitions, for they involve us and our responsibility
before You to the dark world which is moving with terrifying
alacrity toward the end-time; through Jesus Christ, our Lord, who
with You and the Holy Spirit are one God with dominion over us
forever.

C

Lesson II: Revelation 22:12-17, 20

Blessed Lord and Savior Jesus Christ, who has redeemed us from
perdition and who has invited and welcomed us into the Kingdom
of Grace, keep us ready for Your invitation to glory and hold us
steady at the moment of Your glorious appearing; who with the
Father and the Holy Spirit are one God with dominion over us
forever.

Lesson I: Acts 16:6-10
The Gospel: John 17:20-26

Eternal God, whose holy will and love have been demonstrated in
the death and resurrection of Jesus Christ, our Lord, so fill our
hearts and minds that we love You above all things and our
neighbor as ourselves with such telling effect that in us Your love is
made visible to the world; through Jesus Christ, our Lord, who
with You and the Holy Spirit are one God with dominion over us
forever.

The Day of Pentecost

Lesson II: Acts 2:1-21

Holy Spirit, who strengthened the heart of Simon Peter to preach Jesus Christ on the day of Your appearing at Jerusalem, embolden us whom You have also called to faith, to speak the saving Word, and then open the hearts of all who hear it, that they may be brought to the kingdom of God; through Jesus Christ, our Lord, who with You and the Father are one God with dominion over us forever.

Or

Pour out Your power upon us, O Holy Spirit, Creator and Preserver of the faith, that we may be eager instruments in Your plan by which the Good News of redemption is carried to the uttermost parts of the earth; through Jesus Christ, our Lord, who with You and the Father are one God with dominion over us forever.

Or

Holy Comforter, Spirit of truth, who calls, gathers, enlightens, and sanctifies the whole Christian church on earth, though we say it in a thousand languages, our unity in Jesus Christ transcends our diversity of tongues as we bring You praise for Your generosity in one voice this day of the church's founding; through Jesus Christ, our Lord, who with You and the Father are one God with dominion over us forever.

Lesson I: Joel 2:28-29
The Gospel: John 20:19-23

Holy and blessed Spirit, who was sent to us by Christ, our Lord, to call us to and to hold us in the faith, keep us conscious of Your presence in us as we move in mission to the world in obedience to our Lord Christ's mandate to evangelize all people; through Jesus Christ, our Lord, who with You and the Father are one God with dominion over us forever.

B

Lesson II: Acts 2:1-21

See A

Lesson I: Ezekiel 37:1-14

The Gospel: John 7:37-39a (" . . . were to receive.")

Holy Spirit, poured out at Pentecost, the power of God for salvation, continue to call, gather, enlighten, and sanctify the whole Christian church on earth that she may be a fitting and proper bride for our Lord who loves her; through Jesus Christ, our Lord, who with You and the Father are one God with dominion over us forever.

C

Lesson II: Acts 2:1-21

See A

Lesson I: Genesis 11:1-9

The Gospel: John 15:26-27; 16:4b-11

Holy Spirit, to whom is assigned the spread of the Good News of Jesus Christ and the election of people to the Kingdom of Grace, receive our thanksgiving for our faith and hope, through which by Your counsel and work we have committed our whole future to our gracious God; through Jesus Christ, our Lord, who with You and the Father are one God with dominion over us forever.

The Holy Trinity
First Sunday After Pentecost

A

Lesson II: 2 Corinthians 13:11-14

Blessed Trinity, three Persons in one divine essence, stay near us continually maintaining the love relationship in the fellowship You have established with us lest we, left to ourselves, inherit damnation; who lives and reigns eternally, one God, with dominion over us forever.

Lesson I
Genesis 1:1—2:3 or Deuteronomy 4:32-34, 39-40
The Gospel: Matthew 28:16-20

King of kings, Lord of lords, whose rule encompasses heaven and earth, lead us to obedience to the discipling mandate, that every person under the dominion of Satan may hear the Gospel and that many by the power of the Spirit change their allegiance to You; who with the Father and the Holy Spirit are one God with dominion over us forever.

B

Lesson II: Romans 8:14-17

Almighty God, Father of our Lord, Jesus Christ, and our Father, since we have been adopted into Your family through Christ's sacrifice and the Spirit's commendation, grant us grace to be loyal and contributing members of it; through Jesus Christ, our Lord, who with You and the Holy Spirit are one God with dominion over us forever.

84

Lesson I: Deuteronomy 6:4-9
The Gospel: John 3:1-17

Blessed Trinity, Father, Son, and Holy Spirit yet one God, who has created, redeemed, and sanctified us, sustain us, who are born of water and the Spirit, in the Kingdom of Grace in order that we do not lose the Kingdom of Glory; who lives and reigns eternally, one God with dominion over us forever.

=================== **C** ===================

Lesson II: Romans 5:1-5

Blessed Trinity, by whom we have been created, justified, and reborn, guide us through all testing and temptations in time until we realize our hope of spending eternity with You; through Jesus Christ, our Lord, who with the Father and the Holy Spirit are one God with dominion over us forever.

Lesson I: Proverbs 8:22-31
The Gospel: John 16:12-15

Holy Spirit, into whose care and keeping the Father of all truth has entrusted the truth of Jesus Christ, open us to that truth, that knowing and trusting in Christ, we may live in the freedom and under the Lordship of Christ; through the same Jesus Christ, our Lord, who with You and the Father are one Lord with dominion over us forever.

Second Sunday After Pentecost

========== **A** ==========

Lesson II
Romans 3:21-25a (" . . . received by faith."), 27-28

Gracious heavenly Father, who exchanged the law of works for the law of faith for the sake of all people, receive our praise that You have declared us righteous in Your Son and thus delivered us from the deceit of self-righteousness; through Jesus Christ, our Lord, who with You and the Holy Spirit are one God with dominion over us forever.

Lesson I: Deuteronomy 11:18-21, 26-28
The Gospel: Matthew 7:(15-20) 21-29

Holy Spirit, Guarantor of the faith, guide us to obey Your Word and so to share in its promises; through Jesus Christ, our Lord, who with You and the Father are one God with dominion over us forever.

========== **B** ==========

Lesson II: 2 Corinthians 4:5-12

Holy Spirit, whose business is the dissemination of the Gospel and the conferring of faith and commitment to Jesus Christ, sustain us fragile vessels entrusted to be Your servants in the task of proclaiming the Good News and give us faith enough that we always consider ourselves expendable in the doing of it; through Jesus Christ, our Lord, who with You and the Father are one God with dominion over us forever.

Lesson I: Deuteronomy 5:12-15
The Gospel: Mark 2:23-28

Gracious God, Lord of every son and daughter of heaven, whose love triumphed over justice and whose mercy supersedes Your wrath, endlessly remind us that in Christ our Savior works are the fruit of faith lest we, trusting in our works, lose the faith and so identify ourselves as children of the first Adam rather than the Second; through Jesus Christ, our Lord, who with You and the Holy Spirit are one God with dominion over us forever.

C

Lesson II: Galatians 1:1-10

Holy Spirit, Keeper of the key, Guardian of the Gospel, hold us all faithful to the Good News of Jesus Christ, lest we lose it, or deny it, or reject it, and so forfeit the hope of eternal life as well; through Jesus Christ, our Lord, who with You and the Father are one God with dominion over us forever.

Lesson I: 1 Kings 8:(22-23, 27-30), 41-43
The Gospel: Luke 7:1-10

Gracious God, who effected our salvation through our Mediator and Advocate, bless us with courage and purpose to be mediators of the Good News of Jesus Christ to all the world and willing servants to every neighbor; through Jesus Christ, our Lord, who with You and the Holy Spirit are one God with dominion over us forever.

Third Sunday After Pentecost

A

Lesson II: Romans 4:18-25

God of the patriarchs, Lord of our fathers, whom Abraham served without wavering, strengthen our faith and trust in Jesus Christ to such dimensions that no trial or temptation can dissuade us from our single-minded commitment to You; through Jesus Christ, our Lord, who with You and the Holy Spirit are one God with dominion over us forever.

Lesson I: Hosea 5:15—6:6
The Gospel: Matthew 9:9-13

Jesus Christ, who suffered and died for us sinners, alert us to answer Your call to follow You, and keep us from using our sinfulness as an excuse when You lead us to service to our neighbor or to martyrdom; who with the Father and the Spirit are one God with dominion over us forever.

B

Lesson II: 2 Corinthians 4:13-18

Almighty God, heavenly Father, whose curse destroys, whose blessing restores, cover us with Your wings, support us by Your power, hold us in Your hand as we move through life, that we may receive the home eternal when our life has run its course; through Jesus Christ, our Lord, who with You and the Holy Spirit are one God with dominion over us forever.

Lesson I: Genesis 3:9-15
The Gospel: Mark 3:20-35

Jesus Christ, in whose power all creation subsists, keep us from ever being hedged in by Your humanity and thus losing our salvation, but by the Spirit's mighty power hold our eyes on Your deity and our promised eternity with You; who with the Father and the Holy Spirit are one God with dominion over us forever.

C

Lesson II: Galatians 1:11-24

Holy Spirit of the Godhead, to whom the dispensing of the Good News of the redemption of the world through Jesus Christ, our Lord, has been charged, guide every person confronted by a choice between the traditions of the fathers and salvation through Jesus Christ to select Christ as Lord, that his eternity in glory be assured and his purposes in life be oriented to the building of Christ's kingdom; through the same Jesus Christ, our Lord, who with You and the Father are one God with dominion over us forever.

Lesson I: 1 Kings 17:17-24
The Gospel: Luke 7:11-17

Holy God, in whose hands are the issues of life and death for every person, we commit our mortality to Your wisdom and plan and our immortality to Your loving care with the prayer that while we are living in time we may be the Holy Spirit's instruments for bringing new life to all the spiritually dead whose lives touch ours; through Jesus Christ, our Lord, who with You and the Holy Spirit are one God with dominion over us forever.

Fourth Sunday After Pentecost

A

Lesson II: Romans 5:6-11

Lord Jesus Christ, who in love for us endured the righteous wrath of God which was against us for our sins, we hold the reconciliation You thus effected between God and us as our greatest treasure and our highest joy; who with the Father and the Holy Spirit are one God with dominion over us forever.

Lesson I: Exodus 19:2-8a (" . . . we will do.")
The Gospel: Matthew 9:35—10:8

Lord Jesus Christ, who was sent into time, into our world, to accomplish our redemption, make us to realize that we have been called in time at Your will and order to be sent to all the world to speak to it Your reconciling Word; who with the Father and the Holy Spirit are one God with dominion over us forever.

B

Lesson II: 2 Corinthians 5:1-10

Holy Spirit, whose call included us in the holy faith, and whose enlightenment through the Gospel holds us in it, keep us from falling and failing in the testing time in which we must live by faith until we come home at last; through Jesus Christ, our Lord, who with You and the Father are one God with dominion over us forever.

Lesson I: Ezekiel 17:22-24
The Gospel: Mark 4:26-34

Holy Spirit, whose Kingdom building moves on its relentless course toward its end-time completion, make strong our faith and trust when we fail to see Your plan and progress, lest we despair and denounce it and be forced to watch the end-time splendor from afar; through Jesus Christ, our Lord, who with You and the Father are one God with dominion over us forever.

C

Lesson II: Galatians 2:11-21

Blessed Jesus, Very God of Very God, Lord and Ruler of all creation, Redeemer of the world, cast out all that is unworthy in us and fill us with Yourself, that all our thoughts and all the actions proceeding from them might be evidence of Your living presence in us; who with the Father and the Holy Spirit are one God with dominion over us forever.

Lesson I: 2 Samuel 11:26—12:10, 13-15
The Gospel: Luke 7:36-50

Heavenly Father, who through the death of Jesus Christ has made forgiveness possible for all people, and who through the Holy Spirit has affirmed our forgiveness, accept our praise and thanksgiving, for they are brought and laid before You in our profoundest and most grateful love; through Jesus Christ, our Lord, who with You and the Holy Spirit are one God with dominion over us forever.

Fifth Sunday After Pentecost

A

Lesson II: Romans 5:12-15

Heavenly Father, Lord of life and death, who for the trespasses of Adam placed all humanity under judgment and who through the grace of Jesus Christ has supplanted that judgment with new life, let a clear proclamation of such wondrous good news be made to all people that they may hear and by the power of the Spirit believe it; through Jesus Christ, our Lord, who with the Father and the Holy Spirit are one God with dominion over us forever.

Lesson I: Jeremiah 20:7-13
The Gospel: Matthew 10:24-33

Omniscient Lord, who notes the falling hair and the weary sparrow, strengthen our faith for our weak and fearful moments lest our burden be more than our trust will bear; through Jesus Christ, our Lord, who with You and the Holy Spirit are one God with dominion over us forever.

B

Lesson II: 2 Corinthians 5:14-21

Lord Jesus Christ, who died for our sins and rose again for our justification, so fill us with Yourself that all our being is under Your control, so let us by faith be in You that we be dead to ourselves and altogether new creatures whose love and obedience bring praise and honor to You alone; who with the Father and the Holy Spirit are one God with dominion over us forever.

Lesson I: Job 38:1-11
The Gospel: Mark 4:35-41

Jesus Christ, Lord of the wind and the waves, comfort us in the vicissitudes of life, protect us in all times of trial, console us in all times of grief, and reassure us in all times of fear, that our passage to the safe harbor be made with us remembering that You are Captain of our ship; who with the Father and the Holy Spirit are one God with dominion over us forever.

C

Lesson II: Galatians 3:23-29

Lord Jesus Christ, Healer of division and Core of the Christian family, give us grace through the indwelling Spirit to see all other persons through Your eyes, that we may forgive them, love them, and gladly include them in this Your community of which You have made us a part; who with the Father and the Spirit are one God with dominion over us forever.

Lesson I: Zechariah 12:7-10
The Gospel: Luke 9:18-24

Holy Spirit, who, dwelling in us, makes it possible to affirm Jesus Christ, our Lord, daily cause us to deny ourselves and take up our cross to follow Him, for we would lose our lives for His sake; through Jesus Christ, our Lord, who with You and the Father are one God with dominion over us forever.

Sixth Sunday After Pentecost

══════════ A ══════════

Lesson II: Romans 6:1b-11 ("Are we to . . . ")

Almighty and holy God, we pray You who have seen us pass through death with Christ in the holy waters of our baptism, teach us to live for You after the example of Christ in this new life given to us by the Spirit; through Jesus Christ, our Lord, who with You and the Holy Spirit are one God with dominion over us forever.

Lesson I: Jeremiah 28:5-9
The Gospel: Matthew 10:34-42

O Lord Jesus, by whose resurrection eternal life is guaranteed to all believers, give us the wisdom, courage, and strength necessary to honor and serve You above all else; who with the Father and the Holy Spirit are one God with dominion over us forever.

══════════ B ══════════

Lesson II: 2 Corinthians 8:1-9, 13-14

Heavenly Father, to whom belong all the silver and gold and the cattle on a thousand hills, by Your love and the love of Christ motivate us to loving concern for those less fortunate than we, and elevate our stewardship until it is a true expression of our gratitude to You; through Jesus Christ, our Lord, who with You and the Holy Spirit are one God with dominion over us forever.

Lesson I: Lamentations 3:22-33
The Gospel: Mark 5:21-24a, 35-43 or Mark 5:24b-34

Jesus, Sovereign of life, who healed the sick and forgave sins, for giving us life where there was no life and hope where there was no hope, we tender deepest gratitude as we press on from life to life and stand on tiptoe awaiting the fulfillment of our hopes; who with the Father and the Holy Spirit are one God with dominion over us forever.

C

Lesson II: Galatians 5:1, 13-25

Heavenly Father, who hates evil, yet loves the sinner, receive our gratitude for our freedom from the condemning Law and our escape from Your judgment through Jesus Christ, our Redeemer and Liberator, and preserve us from all temptation to deny or betray Him by word or deed; through the same Jesus Christ, our Lord, who with You and the Holy Spirit are one God with dominion over us forever.

Lesson I: 1 Kings 19:14-21
The Gospel: Luke 9:51-62

Holy Spirit, Builder and Keeper of the Kingdom of Grace, grant us, whom You have called into discipleship of Christ, a commitment strong enough to carry us to the death for Him if the necessity arises; through Jesus Christ, our Lord, who with You and the Father are one God with dominion over us forever.

Seventh Sunday After Pentecost

═══ A ═══

Lesson II: Romans 7:15-25a

Gracious Lord Jesus, who rescued us from the due and just reward of our sins, we pray that our appreciation for our freedom from the Law and its condemnation may explode into freely given service in Your kingdoms of power and grace; who with the Father and the Holy Spirit are one God with dominion over us forever.

Lesson I: Zechariah 9:9-12
The Gospel: Matthew 11:25-30

Lord Jesus, who has freed us from the tyranny of the Law to live under the glorious Gospel, give us wisdom to rejoice in our new life and grace to live it in ministry to our peers and in praise of Your high and holy name; who with the Father and the Holy Spirit are one God with dominion over us forever.

═══ B ═══

Lesson II: 2 Corinthians 12:7-10

Holy Spirit, to whom belongs the responsibility of faith, give us grace to be strong in our weakness only because of Christ, lest being strong in our own right there be no room for Christ in us and we lose the Kingdom; through Jesus Christ, our Lord, who with You and the Father are one God with dominion over us forever.

Lesson I: Ezekiel 2:1-5
The Gospel: Mark 6:1-6

Holy Spirit, to whom the responsibility of faith belongs, keep us far enough away from Jesus, the Christ, that we see Him as the Son of God and close enough to Him that we find strength and purpose in that knowledge; through Jesus Christ, our Lord, who with You and the Father are one God with dominion over us forever.

C

Lesson II: Galatians 6:1-10, 14-16

Holy Spirit, who in unfathomable decisions elected us to grace, restrain us from glorying in any thing or any one except Jesus Christ for whom we have died to the world and by whom we live again to call the world to repentance and to faith by the Word of God; through Jesus Christ, our Lord, who with You and the Father are one God with dominion over us forever.

Lesson I: Isaiah 66:10-14
The Gospel: Luke 10:1-12, 16 (17-20)

Holy God, heavenly Father, who speaks through Christ who speaks through us, fill us with the Holy Spirit lest by our silence and inaction the progression of Your will to the world is hindered and mankind fail to hear and know it because of us; through Jesus Christ, our Lord, who with You and the Holy Spirit are one God with dominion over us forever.

Eighth Sunday After Pentecost

A

Lesson II: Romans 8:18-25

Lord Jesus, Son of God and Son of Man, glorious object of our end-time hope and expectation, grant us patience to wait for Your appearing, using our talents and our time in obedience to Your will and purpose until You come; who with the Father and the Holy Spirit are one God with dominion over us forever.

Lesson I: Isaiah 55:10-11

The Gospel: Matthew 13:1-9 (18-23)

Lord of the planting and reaping, Husbandman of the Kingdom grainfields, nourish us with Your Holy Word and sacraments, cause us to produce fruit worthy of Your love, and keep us fit for the harvest when it comes; through Jesus Christ, our Lord, who with You and the Father are one God with dominion over us forever.

B

Lesson II: Ephesians 1:3-14

Heavenly Father, whose gracious heart is ever open toward us and whose spiritual gifts are greater than we ask and more than we deserve, make us appreciate the enormity of Your goodness and the extent of Your generosity, that we continually demonstrate our acceptance of them in praise of Your glory and in obedience to Your holy will; through Jesus Christ, our Lord, who with You and the Holy Spirit are one God with dominion over us forever.

Lesson I: Amos 7:10-15

The Gospel: Mark 6:7-13

Holy Spirit, who at the will of Christ came to apply the

redemption to the hearts and souls of people in His day, grant us a continuing vision of the kingdom of God and its blessing to all people and a will to be in mission for it now in our turn that the Kingdom of Grace be offered to all in the family of man and that all the elect in Christ come at last to the Kingdom of Glory; through Jesus Christ, our Lord, who with You and the Father are one God with dominion over us forever.

C

Lesson II: Colossians 1:1-14

Holy Spirit, who blesses us with all spiritual gifts, we thank You for our faith in Jesus Christ, we pray You to help us love our peers, and we praise You for the hope laid up for us in glory; for Your gifts make our days worthwhile and our future with our Lord our greatest expectation; through Jesus Christ, our Savior, who with You and the Father are one God with dominion over us forever.

Lesson I: Deuteronomy 30:9-14
The Gospel: Luke 10:25-37

Beloved Jesus, who comes to us in our times of need to comfort, to strengthen, and to heal us, pressure us by Your compassion for us to be likewise compassionate for every needy fellowman, lest we, passing by unheeding, fail to minister to You; who with the Father and the Spirit are one God with dominion over us forever.

Ninth Sunday After Pentecost

A

Lesson II: Romans 8:26-27

Heavenly Father, who knows our weaknesses and failings, who searches our hearts, behold, now, the Holy Spirit in us who with constant pleading intercedes for us in all times and places when and where we cease our prayers and praying; through Jesus Christ, our Lord, who with You and the Holy Spirit are one God with dominion over us forever.

Lesson I: Isaiah 44:6-8

The Gospel: Matthew 13:24-30 (36-43)

Most worthy Judge eternal, who will separate believers from the faithless at the Last Day, keep us from forever judging who is first for the Kingdom and lead us to minister to others as to people for whom Christ died; through Jesus Christ, our Lord, who with the Father and the Spirit are one God with dominion over us forever.

B

Lesson II: Ephesians 2:13-22

Holy Spirit, by whom the mighty work of Christ is applied to the affairs of men, implant in us the will and the grace to live with Christ, in Christ, by Christ, and for Christ, that we may have His kind of peace with our heavenly Father, and the peace between us and all people that He died to make possible; through Jesus Christ, our Lord, who with You and the Father are one God with dominion over us forever.

Lesson I: Jeremiah 23:1-6

The Gospel: Mark 6:30-34

Lord Jesus, the Christ, since we stand in an endless necessity of learning and growing by Your teaching, and in constant necessity of applying Your teaching to the affairs of our life and living, continue to expose us to Your Word and the power of the Spirit that accompanies it, and to the affairs of life that call for the presence of the Holy Spirit; who with the Father and the Holy Spirit are one God with dominion over us forever.

C

Lesson II: Colossians 1:21-28

Holy Spirit, bless the church in mission that the world may know the meaning of the mystery of Christ, learn to confess Him, and live in the great hope of the glory which can come to it alone through Him; in the name of Jesus Christ, our Lord, who with You and the Father are one God with dominion over us forever.

Lesson I: Genesis 18:1-10a (10b-14)
The Gospel: Luke 10:38-42

Holy Spirit, since You teach us to love both God and neighbor, and since Jesus fulfilled this commandment in His time, save us from hesitating between these two loves to the point of paralysis, and help us to know that both are done at the same time and that it is only a matter of which one shows; through Jesus Christ, our Lord, who with You and the Father are one God with dominion over us forever.

Tenth Sunday After Pentecost

A

Lesson II: Romans 8:28-30

Eternal and omnipotent God, who at the creation of the world made order out of chaos, by Your Holy Spirit teach us to know and trust Your promises, for if we are left to our own devices, we will surely lose our way to the mansions; through Jesus Christ, our Lord, who with You and the Holy Spirit are one God with dominion over us forever.

Lesson I: 1 Kings 3:5-12
The Gospel: Matthew 13:44-52

Lord Jesus Christ, whose knowledge and wisdom is infinite, move all humanity to seek the incomparable treasure of the Kingdom of Grace which You so completely endorsed, that no one lose the incomparable wonder of the Kingdom of Glory promised by the Father to those who own the treasure; who with the Father and the Holy Spirit are one God with dominion over us forever.

B

Lesson II: Ephesians 4:1-7, 11-16

Holy Spirit, in whose dominion is the calling and the sending of God's own people, bind us in our diversity into a unity in Christ, and for Christ send us in our diversity to call mankind to our community for the sake of Christ; through the same Jesus Christ, our Lord, who with You and the Father are one God with dominion over us forever.

Lesson I: Exodus 24:3-11
The Gospel: John 6:1-15

Jesus Christ, Lord of the loaves and the fishes and Champion of all humanity, by faith let us see You behind the miracle of the multiplied bread and fish and through the miracle show us the splendor of Your promised end-time banquet; who with the Father and the Holy Spirit are one God with dominion over us forever.

C

Lesson II: Colossians 2:6-15

Omnipotent God, Creator, Redeemer, Sanctifier, who has given us breath and new life in Christ, teach us to cherish our creation, but far more, teach us to treasure our new life in Christ, guaranteed to us by the Spirit's power in the Word and sacraments by which we live; through Jesus Christ, our Lord, who with the Father and the Spirit are one God with dominion over us forever.

Lesson I: Genesis 18:20-32
The Gospel: Luke 11:1-13

Gracious Father, since in the disclosure of Your great heart by Your Son, Jesus Christ, we have learned to know Your love, Your great concern, Your overwhelming generosity, we do not cease to marvel that we should be the objects of its devotion; through Jesus Christ, our Lord, who with You and the Holy Spirit are one God with dominion over us forever.

Eleventh Sunday After Pentecost

═══════ A ═══════

Lesson II: Romans 8:35-39

Great and gentle Love of our souls, whose love is more constant than the sun, allow nothing to come between us lest we perish in the darkness and the cold; who with the Father and the Holy Spirit are one God with dominion over us forever.

Lesson I: Isaiah 55:1-5

The Gospel: Matthew 14:13-21

Divine Creator and Preserver, who at the prayer of Your Son increased the loaves and fishes, at our prayer be pleased to increase our faith and to bless the Word and break it as nourishment for all the human family; through Jesus Christ, our Lord, who with You and the Holy Spirit are one God with dominion over us forever.

═══════ B ═══════

Lesson II: Ephesians 4:17-24

Holy Spirit, by whose power in the sacred Word the elect are called to faith, guide us, who have learned to know and who have put on Christ, to wear His righteousness with pride and to bear His image to the untutored world in all humility; through the same Jesus Christ, our Lord, who with You and the Father are one God with dominion over us forever.

Lesson I: Exodus: 16:2-15

The Gospel: John 6:24-35

Because our souls ache for spiritual food and yearn for water to abate our spiritual thirst, O Jesus, who is the Living Water and the Bread of Life, lead us to the laden table of Your Word and refresh us with the sparkling water of Your love, for the constant renewing and strengthening of our life in You; who with the Father and the Holy Spirit are one God with dominion over us forever.

C

Lesson II: Colossians 3:1-11

Holy Spirit, who impells us to despair by the terrors of the Law and who by the grace of the Gospel draws us to faith, let Christ so be in us and us so be in Him, that no evil or idolatrous acts darken our lives and that in Him we livè in the image of our glorious Creator; through Jesus Christ, our Lord, who with You and the Father are one God with dominion over us forever.

Lesson I: Ecclesiastes 1:2; 2:18-26
The Gospel: Luke 12:13-21

Divine Wisdom, holy Omniscient One, whose knowledge embraces all things, guide us in all our decisions that they reflect a dependence on and deference to You, so that we do not lose the great treasure of this life or the joys of the life which is to come because of our unreliable self-will; through Jesus Christ, our Lord, who with the Father and the Holy Spirit are one God with dominion over us forever.

Twelfth Sunday After Pentecost

══════════ A ══════════

Lesson II: Romans 9:1-5

Lord Jesus Christ, whose love for every member of the human family is infinite, let Your call to all people to repent and embrace the faith be constant, and keep us, who have been given the gift of faith, from denying or betraying You; who with the Father and the Holy Spirit are one God with dominion over us forever.

Lesson I: 1 Kings 19:9-18
The Gospel: Matthew 14:22-33

Jesus Christ, Son of God, who walked the mountaintops and the cresting waves, stay by our side in sunshine and in storm, for we lack faith and courage enough to face the vicissitudes that life thrusts on us and are so very slow to pray when there are no trials for us to face; who with the Father and the Holy Spirit are one God with dominion over us forever.

══════════ B ══════════

Lesson II: Ephesians 4:30—5:2

Holy Spirit, who has stamped us with Your seal and affixed upon us the guarantee of our righteousness in Christ, enable us, therefore, now to transcend the evil issue of our flesh and to be as kind, as tender, and as forgiving to our fellow sinners as our gracious Lord has been to us; through Jesus Christ, our Lord, who with You and the Father are one God with dominion over us forever.

Lesson I: 1 Kings 19:4-8
The Gospel: John 6:41-51

Jesus, Son of God, enter into our lives that we may enter into

Yours, that thus nourished we may be strong enough to shoulder the burden of servanthood while the light of our day lasts; who with the Father and the Holy Spirit are one God with dominion over us forever.

C

Lesson II: Hebrews 11:1-3, 8-16

Holy Spirit, who dispenses the gracious gifts of the blessed Trinity, we praise You for the breath of life, we glorify You for the faith that brings us the new life in Christ, and we magnify You for the promise of the life to come in the City of God; through Jesus Christ, our Lord, who with You and the Father are one God with dominion over us forever.

Lesson I: Genesis 15:1-6
The Gospel: Luke 12:32-40

Heavenly Father, who in deliberating love has promised us the Kingdom and by the power of the Holy Spirit claimed us for the faith, by that same Spirit sustain us in that faith, that we, seeking Your will above all things, may by Your love inherit that which You have promised; through Jesus Christ, our Lord, who with You and the Holy Spirit are one God with dominion over us forever.

Thirteenth Sunday After Pentecost

A

Lesson II: Romans 11:13-15, 29-32

Eternal Judge, eternal Refuge, who has judged all of us to be disobedient and deserving of death, we praise You for Your mercy in Christ Jesus so freely extended to each of us, and we pray that all people may be led to know, to experience, and to cherish Your mercy; through Jesus Christ, our Lord, who with You and the Holy Spirit are one God with dominion over us forever.

Lesson I: Isaiah 56:1, 6-8

The Gospel: Matthew 15:21-28

Lord God, Healer and Helper of all, grant us love and faith enough to keep us persistent in our prayers for all the hurting and helpless people of the world; through Jesus Christ, our Lord, who with You and the Holy Spirit are one God with dominion over us forever.

B

Lesson II: Ephesians 5:15-20

Let us be Your temple indeed, Holy Spirit of the Godhead, that out of our hearts and lives may flow all things pleasing to the Father who has loved us with all the love of His great God heart; through Jesus Christ, our Lord, who with You and the Father are one God with dominion over us forever.

Lesson I: Proverbs 9:1-6

The Gospel: John 6:51-58

Heavenly Father, Lord of heaven and earth, guide us by Your Spirit and maintain us in the faith in Your Son, the Christ, while we are here in time that we do not lose the prospect of life with You in glory; through Jesus Christ, our Lord, who with You and the Holy Spirit are one God with dominion over us forever.

C

Lesson II: Hebrews 12:1-13

Abba, Father, who provides food and shelter for our frail bodies and trembling souls, as Your children we ask You to continue our training with love and caring discipline that we mature in faith and life; through Jesus Christ, our Lord, who with You and the Holy Spirit are one God with dominion over us forever.

Lesson I: Jeremiah 23:23-29
The Gospel: Luke 12:49-53

Heavenly Father, who made all nations of one blood to dwell together peaceably on earth, forgive us for allowing the division perpetrated by Satan, help us to bridge the Satanic division with Christlike love for every fellow human, and give us patience and persistence with all who have not accepted Christ, for Christ's sake, for their sake, and for ours; through the same Jesus Christ, our Lord, who with You and the Spirit are one God with dominion over us forever.

Fourteenth Sunday After Pentecost

— A —

Lesson II: Romans 11:33-36

Christ Jesus, Son of God and Friend of man, shield us from the fearful awesomeness of God and preserve us from death by terror before Him, by interposing Yourself between Him and us in such a way that we may see His love and live in peace with Him; who with the Father and the Holy Spirit are one God with dominion over us forever.

Lesson I: Exodus 6:2-8
The Gospel: Matthew 16:13-20

Holy Spirit, Caller, Gatherer, Enlightener, Keeper, maintain the answer to the question of Christ in our hearts that we may know aright who we are in Him and be so motivated by such knowledge that our life and example may lead others to glorify our gracious Father; through Jesus Christ, our Lord, who with You and the Father are one God with dominion over us forever.

— B —

Lesson II: Ephesians 5:21-31

Heavenly Father, who created man and woman in Your likeness and in marriage made them one flesh, teach all who live in marriage the obedience and commitment of Christ, that both may bring a willingness to serve and a determination to love to the covenant they have made with each other; through Jesus Christ, our Lord, who with You and the Holy Spirit are one God with dominion over us forever.

Lesson I
Joshua 24:1-2a (" . . . all the people:"), 14-18
The Gospel: John 6:60-69

Jesus, Son of Man, who came from God and went to God, maintain the power of the Spirit in Your Word and thus sustain our faith, lest our commitment falter and we be left on the wayside of the road to glory; who with the Father and the Holy Spirit are one God with dominion over us forever.

C

Lesson II: Hebrews 12:18-24

Gracious Father, from whose hand has come the bounty of spiritual gifts which shape our destiny, steady our sights on the excitement already here and on that which is yet to come, and free us from the temptation to look back at the darkness behind us, for fear of losing our citizenship in the heavenly Jerusalem; through Jesus Christ, our Lord, who with You and the Holy Spirit are one God with dominion over us forever.

Lesson I: Isaiah 66:18-23
The Gospel: Luke 13:22-30

Heavenly Father, whose holy angels guard the gates of heaven, be standing there to recognize and give us entrance when the summons is sent to us, for we will be trusting only in the Son You sent to be our Savior; through the same Jesus Christ, our Lord, who with You and the Holy Spirit are one God with dominion over us forever.

Fifteenth Sunday After Pentecost

A

Lesson II: Romans 12:1-8

Holy Spirit, by whose power we are moved to good works, give us the wisdom and the grace to use the gifts You have given us for the welfare of our neighbor, that the health of the body of Christ be maintained and the people of the world be served in our time; through Jesus Christ, our Lord, who with You and the Father are one God with dominion over us forever.

Lesson I: Jeremiah 15:15-21
The Gospel: Matthew 16:21-26

Holy Spirit, who initiates and maintains faith by the very Word of God, sustain us in our always tenuous trust, that our lives may count for Christ in time even as we count on Christ for eternity; through Jesus Christ, our Lord, who with You and the Father are one God with dominion over us forever.

B

Lesson II: Ephesians 6:10-20

Holy Spirit, Leader of the church militant and Equipper of saints, arm us well for our continuing struggle with the forces of evil that surround us, that in Your power and under Your leadership we may hold and advance the Kingdom for our Lord in whatever situation You place us; through Jesus Christ, our Lord, who with You and the Father are one God with dominion over us forever.

Lesson I: Deuteronomy 4:1-2, 6-8
The Gospel: Mark 7:1-8, 14-15, 21-23

Heavenly Father, from whose heart flows justice and mercy,

cleanse our hearts of all evil and let them bring forth the virtues of the Holy Spirit that our lives may grace the kingdom of Christ, our Lord; through the same Jesus Christ, our Lord, who with You and the Holy Spirit are one God with dominion over us forever.

C

Lesson II: Hebrews 13:1-8

Merciful and gracious Father in heaven, who for the death and resurrection of Jesus Christ has adopted us to be Your sons and daughters, teach us to face our vicissitudes and trials with the same courage and trust with which Christ faced the cross, knowing that all adversity is sifted through Your fingers before You allow it to touch us; through Jesus Christ, our Lord, who with You and the Holy Spirit are one God with dominion over us forever.

Lesson I: Proverbs 25:6-7
The Gospel: Luke 14:1, 7-14

Benevolent Father, gracious God, Host at the end-time banquet for all who are in Christ, stay us from pride in our faith and life, and give us enough insight into Christ to follow His example of servanthood to all; through the same Jesus Christ, our Lord, who with You and the Holy Spirit are one God with dominion over us forever.

Sixteenth Sunday After Pentecost

A

Lesson II: Romans 13:1-10

From of old You have established that all divine and human relationships should be of love, Almighty God, therefore teach us to love You and to love our neighbor as well and so fulfill Your Law; through Jesus Christ, our Lord, who with the Father and the Holy Spirit are one God with dominion over us forever.

Lesson I: Ezekiel 33:7-9
The Gospel: Matthew 18:15-20

Lord Jesus Christ, who placed the keys of the Kingdom into our trembling hands and taught us to forgive those who trespass against us but to hold responsible those who do not repent, give us the wisdom to apply Your Word faithfully and so to use the keys wisely and well; who with the Father and the Holy Spirit are one God with dominion over us forever.

Or

Eternal King, who is more ready to forgive than to condemn, make us so appreciative of our own forgiveness that we are never guilty of an unforgiving heart; who with the Father and the Holy Spirit are one God with dominion over us forever.

B

Lesson II: James 1:17-22 (23-25), 26-27

Blessed Father in heaven, Judge of our motives and deeds, cause our hearts to be faith-full of Christ and our lives love-full as a result, that the issue of our hearts and lives may honor You and be a blessing to others; through Jesus Christ, our Lord, who with You and the Holy Spirit are one God with dominion over us forever.

Lesson I: Isaiah 35:4-7a (" . . . springs of water.")
The Gospel: Mark 7:31-37

Lord Jesus Christ, Ruler of the realm of nature, Healer of our mortal bodies, Redeemer of our eternal souls, still the trembling earth and tempestuous seas when lives are at stake, heal bodies when life and livelihood are threatened, but always according to Your divine purpose, and by the power of the Spirit hold us steadfast in the saving faith until the Judgment; who with the Father and the Holy Spirit are one God with dominion over us forever.

C

Lesson II: Philemon 1 (2-9), 10-21

Heavenly Father, who sees us all as creatures to be loved, help us to love beyond the barriers of our culture, our social status, our economic situation, our race, and our creed, that the love which we profess and practice may more nearly match Yours; through Jesus Christ, our Lord, who with You and the Holy Spirit are one God with dominion over us forever.

Lesson I: Proverbs 9:8-12
The Gospel: Luke 14:25-33

Holy Spirit, to whose charge the keeping of the faith in the hearts of God's people is given, grant us such a single-minded devotion to Christ that no other love or loyalty can tempt us from the course on which You have set us; through Jesus Christ, our Lord, who with You and the Father are one God with dominion over us forever.

Seventeenth Sunday After Pentecost

A

Lesson II: Romans 14:5-9

Blessed Jesus, who, deigning to share the Father with us, has become our Brother, know our grateful hearts that when we live, You are our Champion and Hope and when we die, You are our Comfort and Friend; who with the Father and the Holy Spirit are one God with dominion over us forever.

Lesson I: Genesis 50:15-21
The Gospel: Matthew 18:21-35

Gracious God, as You maintain the purity of the Kingdom of Grace by constant forgiveness because of Christ, so help us to purify the community of saints by constant forgiveness like Yours, each to the other of us because of Christ; who with You and the Holy Spirit are one God with dominion over us forever.

B

Lesson II: James 2:1-5, 8-10, 14-18

Holy Spirit, to whom is charged the distribution of faith in Jesus Christ and the power for Christian living, keep us from using faith as an excuse for neglecting the life to which trusting in Christ, the reigning Lord, commits us; through Jesus Christ, our Lord, who with You and the Father are one God with dominion over us forever.

Lesson I: Isaiah 50:4-10
The Gospel: Mark 8:27-35

Heavenly Father, who demanded commitment even to the death of your Son, Jesus Christ, give us understanding of His purposes in such measure that we, too, are willing to expend the price of faith and the cost of the Christian life in sheer gratitude to You and to Him; through Jesus Christ, our Lord, who with You and the Holy Spirit are one God with dominion over us forever.

C

Lesson II: 1 Timothy 1:12-17

Out of Your mercy and grace, O Lord of hosts, You have given mercy and grace even to those who live in ignorance and unbelief, that, finding forgiveness in Jesus Christ, they may be examples to the world of Your unbounded love for it; through Jesus Christ, our Lord, who with You and the Holy Spirit are one God with dominion over us forever.

Lesson I: Exodus 32:7-14
The Gospel: Luke 15:1-10

Ever-present and allwise Lord, who has promised to be with us in all circumstances, help us to remember constantly that Your love transcends our unlovableness, and that Your concern and mercy follow us, even and especially when we are lost; through Jesus Christ, our Lord, who with You and the Spirit are one God with dominion over us forever.

Eighteenth Sunday After Pentecost

===== A =====

Lesson II: Philippians 1:1-5, (6-11), 19-27

Holy Spirit, Sanctifier of our souls, purge us of every obstacle to Christ's living in us that we may live and die in Christ; through Jesus Christ, our Lord, who with You and the Father are one God with dominion over us forever.

Lesson I: Isaiah 55:6-9
The Gospel: Matthew 20:1-16

Lord Jesus, who rules in equity and who gives to each his due, sustain us in the day's heat and contain us at the day's end, that we show ourselves appreciative of Your grace and zealous for Your glory; who with the Father and the Holy Spirit are one God with dominion over us forever.

===== B =====

Lesson II: James 3:16—4:6

Holy Christ, whose death and resurrection made our peace with God possible again, fill us with such trust and wisdom that purity, peacefulness, openness, mercy, and conviction continually mark our lives and conversation; who with the Father and the Holy Spirit are one God with dominion over us forever.

Lesson I: Jeremiah 11:18-20
The Gospel: Mark 9:30-37

Holy Spirit of the Godhead, who has called us into the marvelous light of Christ, lead us also in the footsteps of Christ that the sinner in us always give way to our sainthood in Christ; through that same

Jesus Christ, our Lord, who with You and the Father are one God with dominion over us forever.

C

Lesson II: 1 Timothy 2:1-8

Holy Spirit, by whose power in the Word and sacraments alone Jesus can be called Lord, move many through these means to acknowledge Him Lord; through Jesus Christ, our Lord, who with You and the Father are one God with dominion over us forever.

Lesson I: Amos 8:4-7
The Gospel: Luke 16:1-13

Heavenly Father, to whom belongs the wisdom of the ages, guide us to decisions that comfort us, but more than any other, guide us to Yourself, lest having great comfort here we forfeit the glory to come; through Jesus Christ, our Lord, who with You and the Holy Spirit are one God with dominion over us forever.

Nineteenth Sunday After Pentecost

A

Lesson II: Philippians 2:1-5 (6-11)

Lord Jesus Christ, who is the motivating incentive of each of us and the cohesive force of our Christian community, keep us aware of Your constant ministry to us that we may stay aware of and fulfill our ministry to each other and thus bring strength to our community; who with the Father and the Holy Spirit are one God with dominion over us forever.

Lesson I: Ezekiel 18:1-4, 25-32
The Gospel: Matthew 21:28-32

Eternal God, whose will must be acknowledged and whose desire must be obeyed lest we perish, free us from ourselves for repentance, fill us from Yourself with faith, and guide us in our reconciliation into all good works; through Jesus Christ, our Lord, who with You and the Holy Spirit are one God with dominion over us forever.

B

Lesson II: James 4:7-12 (13—5:6)

Almighty God, Lawgiver and Judge, who in Christ has blessed us beyond our deserving with forgiveness, life, and hope, grant that we pass on Your gifts in our conduct with all our fellow creatures, that by our example of holy living and our witness to the Gospel they may find and glorify You; through Jesus Christ, our Lord, who with You and the Holy Spirit are one God with dominion over us forever.

Lesson I: Numbers 11:4-6, 10-16, 24-29
The Gospel: Mark 9:38-50

Heavenly Father, who metes out justice on the basis of faith in Your Son, Jesus Christ, give us wisdom to order our lives by the cross which is behind us and by the end-time which lies before us, that we, though losing the world now, may gain heaven for all eternity when our judgment comes; through Jesus Christ, our Lord, who with You and the Holy Spirit are one God with dominion over us forever.

C

Lesson II: 1 Timothy 6:6-16

Holy Spirit, to whom the transmission of the sacred faith is delegated by the councils of the Trinity, keep our generation faithful to Your trust that the generation that follows us may in its turn inherit the Good News of Jesus Christ into its keeping; through the same Jesus Christ, our Lord, who with You and the Father are one God with dominion over us forever.

Lesson I: Amos 6:1-7
The Gospel: Luke 16:19-31

Heavenly Father, restrain us from believing that the voices of the dead or the messages of angels or anything other than Your Word and sacraments, with the power of the Holy Spirit in them, will bring us to, or keep us in, Your holy and saving faith; through Jesus Christ, our Lord, who with You and the Holy Spirit are one God with dominion over us forever.

Twentieth Sunday After Pentecost

Lesson II: Philippians 3:12-21

Jesus Christ, Lord of heaven and earth, who reigns in splendor in the kingdom of heaven, hold the vision of glory ever before us; and as we press on toward it, trusting in Your faithfulness, help us to match our lives to the level of our faith, until by Your grace we see You; who with the Father and the Holy Spirit are one God with dominion over us forever.

Lesson I: Isaiah 5:1-7
The Gospel: Matthew 21:33-43

Almighty God, who is at once our Judge and Justifier, by the power of the Holy Spirit open our spiritual eyes to the Christ who came and comes, lest we, failing to recognize Your only begotten Son and our Redeemer, reject Him and perish eternally; through Jesus Christ, our Lord, who with You and the Holy Spirit are one God with dominion over us forever.

== B ==

Lesson II: Hebrews 2:9-11 (12-18)

Heavenly Father, whose Son is Jesus Christ our Savior, and whose we are by adoption through Your Son's vicarious satisfaction for us, let us neither shame nor deny our Brother in our daily round of living but rather glory in the honor and privilege of having Christ for Brother and being Your adopted children; through Jesus Christ, our Lord, who with You and the Holy Spirit are one God with dominion over us forever.

Lesson I: Genesis 2:18-24
The Gospel: Mark 10:2-16

Lord Jesus, Savior, who by a cross overcame sin and death and Satan and by whose cross the alienation of people to each other is healed, let the cross be our sure bridge to every person, and theirs to us, to gain in some measure again the blessed relationship originally enjoyed in Eden; who with the Father and the Holy Spirit are one God with dominion over us forever.

C

Lesson II: 2 Timothy 1:3-14

Holy Spirit, Dispenser of the faith which is in Jesus Christ, since You have entrusted us with the saving faith, empower us to boldly live and proclaim it, that the means through which You call people to it may be available to our generation and those yet to come; through Jesus Christ, our Lord, who with You and the Father are one God with dominion over us forever.

Lesson I: Habakkuk 1:1-3; 2:1-4
The Gospel: Luke 17:1-10

Heavenly Father, who persistently rebukes and forgives us, teach us to be so constant in forgiving our offending and repentant brothers and sisters that there may be peace between us as reassuring as the peace Your forgiveness affords us; through Jesus Christ, our Lord, who with You and the Holy Spirit are one God with dominion over us forever.

Twenty-first Sunday After Pentecost

═══ A ═══

Lesson II: Philippians 4:4-13

Almighty Trinity, who because You created us also understand us, and who understanding us gave us faith, and who dwelling in us gives us strength to face life's crises, we thank You, and pray You never let us forget; who lives and reigns, one God, with dominion over us forever.

Lesson I: Isaiah 25:6-9

The Gospel: Matthew 22:1-10 (11-14)

Lead us to critical self-examination, Lord of the eternal feast, so that we appreciate our invitation to Your forgiveness and eternity, and are better able to help our fellow sinners understand its implications when the invitation comes to them; who with the Father and the Holy Spirit are one God with dominion over us forever.

═══ B ═══

Lesson II: Hebrews 3:1-6

Almighty God, heavenly Father, who has adopted us to be sons and daughters of Your household through Your Son and our Brother Jesus, the Christ, open to us opportunities of service that we may show our love and gratitude and through which we can minister to each other and also to those who are outside the household of faith against the time of their adoption; through Jesus Christ, our Lord, who with You and the Holy Spirit are one God with dominion over us forever.

Lesson I: Amos 5:6-7, 10-15

The Gospel: Mark 10:17-27 (28-30)

Our Father in heaven, who demands and has claim to our total being, if we are holding back any of that which belongs to You, forgive us, and in Your very forgiveness inspire us to release our grasp on it until we are altogether Yours; through Jesus Christ, our Lord, who with You and the Holy Spirit are one God with dominion over us forever.

C

Lesson II: 2 Timothy 2:8-13

Blessed Lord Jesus Christ, David's Son, crucified and risen from the grave, sustain us in our hours of peril and our times of doubt and hold us steady to our trust that we may live and reign with You, even as You promised; who with the Father and the Holy Spirit are one God with dominion over us forever.

Lesson I: Ruth 1:1-19a (" . . . came to Bethlehem.")
The Gospel: Luke 17:11-19

Gracious God, who in grace and mercy supplies our temporal needs, give us faith to await Your gifts and a spirit of thanksgiving whether they come or not, for by Your wisdom we have been chosen to live eternally; through Jesus Christ, our Lord, who with You and the Holy Spirit are one God with dominion over us forever.

Twenty-second Sunday After Pentecost

Lesson II
1 Thessalonians 1:1-5a (" . . . conviction.")

Eternal and sovereign Lord, whose ways and wonders are beyond understanding and past finding out, we say our thanks to You for the election to grace of all our fellow members in Christ and plead with You that many may yet be called into Your Kingdom with us; through Jesus Christ, our Lord, who with You and the Holy Spirit are one God with dominion over us forever.

Lesson I: Isaiah 45:1-7

The Gospel: Matthew 22:15-21

Lord Christ, who rules the nations and the church, grant us who live in the one by birth and the other by faith the wisdom to know the difference between them and the commitment to help each to serve the other without compromising You as Lord of both; who with the Father and the Holy Spirit are one God with dominion over us forever.

—————————— B ——————————

Lesson II: Hebrews 4:9-16

Holy Spirit, who by the Word of God exposes our innermost being, by the same Word close and heal our wounds that it may be said of us that the surgery was successful and the patient lived; through Jesus Christ, our Lord, who with You and the Father are one God with dominion over us forever.

Lesson I: Isaiah 53:10-12

The Gospel: Mark 10:35-45

Holy God, heavenly Father, whose mighty arm strengthens Your people and whose hand holds them steady in all tribulation, be with us when we drink the cup of suffering, give us willingness when we are called upon to serve our neighbor, and strengthen us enough in our faith that we might do both with joy for the sake of Christ, our Lord; who with Jesus Christ and the Holy Spirit are one God with dominion over us forever.

C

Lesson II: 2 Timothy 3:14—4:5

Holy Spirit, Author and Keeper of the sacred Word, encourage and guide us into the Scriptures that through them we may learn more about Christ and be trained in righteousness and so be equipped for every good work; through Jesus Christ, our Lord, who with You and the Father are one God with dominion over us forever.

Lesson I: Genesis 32:22-30
The Gospel
Luke 18:1-8a (" . . . vindicate them speedily.")

Heavenly Father, who has promised to hear us when we pray, keep us childlike enough in our faith to persist in our prayers and make us wise enough to know Your answer when it comes, that we do not presume on each other's time; through Jesus Christ, our Lord, who with You and the Holy Spirit are one God with dominion over us forever.

Twenty-third Sunday After Pentecost

A

Lesson II
1 Thessalonians 1:5b-10 ("You know . . .")

Holy Spirit, Lamplighter for Christ, Builder and Guardian of His church, so equip us with faith that our lives and conversation, by following the example of Christ and His apostles, may open the way for You to call and gather a people for our God; through Jesus Christ, our Lord, who with You and the Father are one God with dominion over us forever.

Lesson I: Leviticus 19:1-2, 15-18
The Gospel: Matthew 22:34-40 (41-46)

Heavenly Father, whose love and mercy to us sinners is constant and certain in Christ our Savior and Lord, teach us by the indwelling Spirit to return Your love with all our heart and soul and mind and to emulate Your love in all our daily contacts with other people, that through us they may come to know Your goodness and learn to call You Father; through Jesus Christ our Lord, who with You and the Holy Spirit are one God with dominion over us forever.

B

Lesson II: Hebrews 5:1-10

Heavenly Father, holy Judge, who sent Christ into our humanity that He might be Priest for us, and who has accepted Him as Sacrificial Lamb in our stead, accept our grateful offering of ourselves to You and make us priests who are endlessly interceding for the whole family of man; through Jesus Christ, our Lord, who with You and the Holy Spirit are one God with dominion over us forever.

Lesson I: Jeremiah 31:7-9
The Gospel: Mark 10:46-52

Holy Spirit, by whom the divine record receives its power to save and heal, give us insights into the sacred record that we might find continued healing for our souls in it, and through it be saved eternally; through Jesus Christ, our Lord, who with You and the Father are one God with dominion over us forever.

C

Lesson II: 2 Timothy 4:6-8, 16-18

O Lord, righteous Judge, Protector of Your chosen people, keep us steady in the faith, fighting the good fight, for the crown of righteousness is indeed laid up for us who have loved the Christ's appearing; through the same Jesus Christ, our Lord, who with You and the Holy Spirit are one God with dominion over us forever.

Lesson I: Deuteronomy 10:12-22
The Gospel: Luke 18:9-14

Holy Spirit, whose working place in the plan of the Godhead is faith and life, purify our motives for living after the example of Christ in order that our lives properly honor Christ and glorify the Father; who together are one God with dominion over us forever.

Twenty-fourth Sunday After Pentecost

A

Lesson II: 1 Thessalonians 4:13-14 (15-18)

Lord God, high and lifted up, who alone knows the hour when the end-time trumpet is to sound, we are comforted that all those who died in Christ and we who now live in Him will be summoned together to our places in glory when the hour comes at last; through Jesus Christ, our Lord, who with You and the Holy Spirit are one God with dominion over us forever.

Lesson I: Amos 5:18-24

The Gospel: Matthew 25:1-13

Lord Jesus, Bridegroom of the church, know that we are waiting and watchful for Your coming, for we would be guests at the eternal wedding feast; who with the Father and the Holy Spirit are one God with dominion over us forever.

B

Lesson II: Hebrews 7:23-28

High and holy Priest of God, whose sacrifice at Calvary atoned for the sins of the world and whose intercession at the judgment seat even now assures our security, we are deeply grateful for salvation, and we need Your continuing prayers in our behalf; who with the Father and the Holy Spirit are one God with dominion over us forever.

Lesson I: Deuteronomy 6:1-9

The Gospel: Mark 12:28-34 (35-37)

Holy God, whose Kingdom is marked by love to mankind and limited by mankind's love to You , we praise and thank You for

Your love to us; we profess our love to You and pray that we be helped to love our neighbor; through Jesus Christ, our Lord, who with You and the Holy Spirit are one God with dominion over us forever.

C

Lesson II: 2 Thessalonians 1:1-5, 11-12

God, the Father of Christ, and our Father, cause our faith in Your Christ and our love for You and each other to grow in the midst of all prosperity and every adversity, for we would glorify the name of our Lord Jesus and present You rightly to the world; through Jesus Christ, our Lord, who with You and the Holy Spirit are one God with dominion over us forever.

Lesson I: Exodus 34:5-9
The Gospel: Luke 19:1-10

Heavenly Father, who loved humanity in spite of its rebellious nature, we have only praise and thanksgiving that Your love in Christ reached each of us, and prayers that our love for all people can somehow approximate Yours; through Jesus Christ, our Lord, who with You and the Holy Spirit are one God with dominion over us forever.

Twenty-fifth Sunday After Pentecost

A

Lesson II: 1 Thessalonians 5:1-11

Gracious Lord, to whom belong all times and seasons, lest we be left to Your wrath when this season of grace ends and the time of Your visitation comes, support us all by Your Holy Spirit that we may wait with patience and be ready for Your arrival; through Jesus Christ, our Lord, who with You and the Holy Spirit are one God with dominion over us forever.

Lesson I: Hosea 11:1-4, 8-9
The Gospel: Matthew 25:14-30

Divine Creator, who has made each person on the face of the earth unique, help all people on the earth to share Your unique gifts to them with all others and so honor and glorify You in the process; through Jesus Christ, our Lord, who with You and the Holy Spirit are one God with dominion over us forever.

B

Lesson II: Hebrews 9:24-28

Dearest Lord Jesus, Savior and Friend, who died on the high altar of Calvary, once for all, let the singularity of Your sacrifice remind us that we live in the end-time and must therefore stand ready and eager for Your second appearing; who with the Father and the Holy Spirit are one God with dominion over us forever.

Lesson I: 1 Kings 17:8-16
The Gospel: Mark 12:41-44

Heavenly Father, whose generosity supplies our needs if not our wants, impress upon us that we are poor when we think ourselves independent of Your favor, and truly rich only when a right relationship with You is created by the power of the Holy Spirit; through Jesus Christ, our Lord, who with You and the Holy Spirit are one God with dominion over us forever.

C

Lesson II: 2 Thessalonians 2:13—3:5

Holy Spirit, whose province is the building of the Kingdom, direct our hearts to the love of God and to the steadfastness of Christ, and thus deliver us from the snares of Satan and the wiles of wicked people; through Jesus Christ, our Lord, who with You and the Father are one God with dominion over us forever.

Lesson I: 1 Chronicles 29:10-13
The Gospel: Luke 20:27-38

Holy Spirit, Guardian of the sacred truths, restrain us from fractious questioning of Your sacred revelation and teach us to accept the divine mysteries in faith, for doubt destroys us, but trust, even in its blindness, brings us life; through Jesus Christ, our Lord, who with You and the Father are one God with dominion over us forever.

Twenty-sixth Sunday After Pentecost

================= **A** =================

Lesson II: 1 Thessalonians 2:8-13

Holy Spirit, whose work is the propagation of the faith, make us strong links in the chain of activity by which the Word is disseminated, lest in weakness we frustrate Your plans for the Kingdom's growth; through Jesus Christ, our Lord, who with You and the Father are one God with dominion over us forever.

Lesson I: Malachi 2:1-2, 4-10
The Gospel: Matthew 23:1-12

Mighty Creator, gentle Protector, who neither slumbers nor sleeps, guard us in all challenges to our faith, that we lose neither the adventure nor the Kingdom that our faith affords us; through Jesus Christ, our Lord, who with You and the Holy Spirit are one God with dominion over us forever.

================= **B** =================

Lesson II: Hebrews 10:11-18

Great High Priest, whose sacrifice at Calvary obviated all other sacrifices in its great sufficiency, lead us to use the freedom and the time we have gained through the cross to praise You and to serve our fellowman; who with the Father and the Holy Spirit are one God with dominion over us forever.

Lesson I: Daniel 12:1-3
The Gospel: Mark 13:1-13

Incite us to mission, Holy Spirit, who groans within us and cries to the Father for us, that all who are indicted by their sins may find Christ, their Savior, before the end-time is realized; through Jesus

Christ, our Lord, who with You and the Father are one God with dominion over us forever.

===================== **C** =====================

Lesson II: 2 Thessalonians 3:6-13

Almighty God, divine Creator, by whose Son and Spirit we were given spiritual life, keep us if it be Your will in such good health and strength mentally and physically that we may earn our board and keep, and preserve us, who belong to You, from living in idleness and dependency unless You will it so; through Jesus Christ, our Lord, who with You and the Holy Spirit are one God with dominion over us forever.

Lesson I: Malachi 4:1-2a (" . . . in its wings.")
The Gospel: Luke 21:5-19

Heavenly Father, whose we are and who is ours, guard us in our discipleship against the terrors that haunt the darkness ahead, that we may pass through them in triumph or suffer martyrdom with honor for the sake of Christ, our Lord; who with You and the Holy Spirit are one God with dominion over us forever.

Twenty-seventh Sunday After Pentecost

A

Lesson II: 1 Thessalonians 3:7-13

Eternal Father, whose justice is indisputable throughout all eternity, increase our trust in Christ, Your Son, and deepen our love for all people, that on Judgment Day the marks of faith may be ours and we be numbered with Your saints; through Jesus Christ, our Lord, who with You and the Holy Spirit are one God with dominion over us forever.

Lesson I: Jeremiah 26:1-6
The Gospel: Matthew 24:1-14

Great God, only Guarantor of our eternity, who foreknows the end-time portents, keep us faithful in our time in the face of adversity, that we neither dishonor Your name nor bring disgrace to Your kingdom by our apostasy; through Jesus Christ, our Lord, who with You and the Holy Spirit are one God with dominion over us forever.

B

Lesson II: Hebrews 13:20-21

Great Shepherd of the sheep and lambs, O Christ, Lamb of God who takes away the world's sin and ours, equip us, who accept Your sacrifice, to proclaim to the sinful world the arrival of the Kingdom that the sacrifice announces; who with the Father and the Holy Spirit are one God with dominion over us forever.

Lesson I: Daniel 7:9-10
The Gospel: Mark 13:24-31

Son of Man, who waits the Father's word to leave the throne to meet the saints arriving at the gates of glory, bid us wait in patience for our call, but keep us ready for the journey to the mansions of our heavenly Father; who with the Father and the Holy Spirit are one God with dominion over us forever.

C

Lesson II: 1 Corinthians 15:54-58

Holy God, who reigns in splendor, since You have accomplished our redemption for eternity through Jesus Christ to make us safe when the summons is issued for us, let us gladly abound in good works for You until that great moment comes; through Jesus Christ, our Lord, who with You and the Holy Spirit are one God with dominion over us forever.

Lesson I: Isaiah 52:1-6
The Gospel: Luke 19:11-27

Beloved God, who has carefully distributed talents and abilities to Your people, grant us vision enough to see their value for Your kingdom and courage and determination enough to use them for it, that You need not be ashamed that You have given them to us; through Jesus Christ, our Lord, who with You and the Holy Spirit are one God with dominion over us forever.

Christ the King

Last Sunday After Pentecost

══════ A ══════

Lesson II: 1 Corinthians 15:20-28

Sovereign God, mighty Lord, permit us, we implore You, the ultimate gift of being present in glory when our Lord Christ delivers the Kingdom to You at Your divine plan's end, for we cannot conceive a time or an event of greater significance or majesty in all of Your dealing with Your creation; through Jesus Christ, our Lord, who with You and the Holy Spirit are one God with dominion over us forever.

Lesson I: Ezekiel 34:11-16, 23-24
The Gospel: Matthew 25:31-46

Son of Man, before whom all people of all the nations will stand at the Judgment, increase our love for You that our love for all humanity may be deepened and our ministry to every person be accomplished, and grant that we be counted with the faithful when You come to judge the world; who with the Father and the Holy Spirit are one God with dominion over us forever.

══════ B ══════

Lesson II: Revelation 1:4b-8 ("Grace to you . . .")

Jesus Christ, wounded Lamb and faithful Witness, Firstborn of the dead, and the Ruler of kings on earth, Alpha and Omega, receive our praise and adoration, for Your death has become our life and Your Servanthood our sainthood; Hallelujah! who with the Father and the Holy Spirit are one God with dominion over us forever.

Lesson I: Daniel 7:13-14
The Gospel: John 18:33-37

Jesus, the Christ, King over all kings, preserve us from indifference to Your rule over us, accept our service to Your kingdom, and multiply our witness by word and deed to the kingdoms of this world; who with the Father and the Holy Spirit are one God with dominion over us forever.

C

Lesson II: Colossians 1:13-20

High and holy God, who through Your Son forgives our sins to make us saints and reveals Yourself to us that we may call You Father, who created the whole world for us to live in and who maintains the church that we might have a community to call our own, who engendered hope for the mansions, and who makes peace through the cross of the reconciliation of all things to Yourself, accept our glory and honor, our praise and thanksgiving, our grateful hearts and lives; through Jesus Christ, our Lord, who with You and the Holy Spirit are one God with dominion over us forever.

Lesson I: Jeremiah 23:2-6
The Gospel: Luke 23:35-43

Beloved King Jesus, who was crucified for us, no king has ever ennobled a throne as You dignified Your cross with divine majesty, the beloved and obedient Son of Your Father to the end; who with the Father and the Holy Spirit are one God with dominion over us forever.

Collects for
the
Lesser Festivals

St. Andrew, Apostle

November 30

Blessed Holy Spirit, who set the example of St. Andrew, humanitarian and evangelist, into the sacred record, bless us with Your presence and power to witness in word and deed to the great care and love of God in all the places into which You have set us; through Jesus Christ, our Lord, who with You and the Father are one God with dominion over us forever.

St. Thomas, Apostle

December 21

Gracious Jesus, Way, Truth, Life, supported by Your Word and the power of the Holy Spirit, lead us from all uncertainty to faith, that, like Your servant apostle Thomas we may be so committed to You that we are ready even for martyrdom; who with the Father and the Holy Spirit are one God with dominion over us forever.

St. Stephen, Deacon and Martyr

December 26

Holy Spirit, Paraclete and Comforter of prophets and messengers whom You send to speak the word of judgment and of hope, sustain them in their witness and hold them constant in their faith in all eventualities as You held St. Stephen at his life's end; through Jesus Christ, our Lord, who with You and the Father are one God with dominion over us forever.

St. John, Apostle and Evangelist

December 27

Gracious Lord, through whose Spirit we are led into the great mystery of Your being and will, receive our praise and gratitude for the work of Your servant and apostle John, by whose word and work we are given insight and faith in our Savior and Friend Jesus, the Christ, who with the Father and the Holy Spirit are one God with dominion over us forever.

The Holy Innocents, Martyrs

December 28

God of mercy, whose steadfast love embraces all people, but especially those who rightly call You Lord, we appreciate how You weep at the martyrdom of Your saints, and pray that we hold fast the saving faith should we be called to forfeit life at the hands of evil men; through Jesus Christ, our Lord, who with the Father and the Holy Spirit are one God with dominion over us forever.

New Year's Eve

December 31

Almighty God, Author of time, come to us with Your forgiveness for the sins of the year of our time now passing, receive our gratitude for its many blessings, and hear our pleas for Your abiding presence and benediction for the days that are ahead of us; through Jesus Christ, our Lord, who with the Father and the Holy Spirit are one God with dominion over us forever.

The Name of Jesus

January 1

Lord Jesus Christ, born into the old covenant, Bringer of the new, grant us who are baptized into Your saving name grace to carry it with pride and purpose today and into all the tomorrows of our lives; who with the Father and the Holy Spirit are one God with dominion over us forever.

The Confession of St. Peter

January 18

Holy Spirit, who inspired the heroic faith of St. Peter at Caesarea Philippi, inspire in all Christians an appreciation of their unity in

Christ and a willingness to confess His name to the praise of God and for the salvation of many bought with the blood of Christ; through Jesus Christ, our Lord, who with You and the Father are one God with dominion over us forever.

The Conversion of St. Paul

January 25

Jesus, Lord, by whom Paul was called to be an apostle and for whom he labored mightily in the world, grant us who are called into discipleship zeal for the Kingdom of Grace, that all who live outside the Kingdom be invited to faith and service in it; who with the Father and the Holy Spirit are one God with dominion over us forever.

The Presentation of Our Lord

February 2

Gracious Lord, grant us faith and obedience like Simeon's, that we, knowing You as Savior and Sovereign, may daily stand ready to die in our service to You; who with the Father and the Holy Spirit are one God with dominion over us forever.

St. Matthias, Apostle

February 24

Holy Spirit, to You by whom we have been elected to share in the Kingdom and the glory we speak our gratitude and pray that, as we have been numbered with the disciples of Jesus, we may serve Him in this world, as becomes all who have joined that glorious company; through Jesus Christ, our Lord, who with You and the Father are one God with dominion over us forever.

The Annunciation of Our Lord

March 25

Holy Spirit, gentle Comforter, by whom Jesus, the Christ, became incarnate in the Virgin's womb, open our hearts and lives to Jesus, Son of God, that He may indeed live in us, and that we in our turn bear Him to the world; through Jesus Christ, our Lord, who with You and the Father are one God with dominion over us forever.

St. Mark, Evangelist

April 25

Divine Paraclete, who through the work of Your holy evangelist St. Mark have presented and preserved the Good News of Jesus Christ to the salvation of many souls, give us power and perseverance to speak the saving Word, that the vision of St. Mark be accomplished in our day; through Jesus Christ, our Lord, who with You and the Father are one God with dominion over us forever.

St. Philip and St. James, Apostles

May 1

Heavenly Father, Lord of grace, as Philip and James were separated from their peers to follow Jesus, to learn of Him, and to become His messengers of the Gospel to the world, so empower us whom You have called out of the world into discipleship, that we too might be apostles of the Good News of Jesus Christ to our peers; through Jesus Christ, our Lord, who with You and the Holy Spirit are one God with dominion over us forever.

The Visitation

May 31

Holy Spirit, grant us all the insight and wisdom to recognize the Christ when He comes to visit us, as once Elizabeth knew Him present by Your will in the womb of the Virgin, that our souls, too, magnify Him and rejoice in Him as Lord and Savior; through Jesus Christ, our Lord, who with You and the Father are one God with dominion over us forever.

146

The Nativity of St. John the Baptist

June 24

Holy Spirit of the living God, who with signs and wonders gave John to Elizabeth and Zechariah that he might be the forerunner of Jesus, encourage us who are baptized into the holy faith to herald the Kingdom which has come, and thus to be signs proclaiming the Christ to the uncommitted multitudes of the world; to the glory of Jesus Christ, our Lord, who with You and the Father are one God with dominion over us forever.

St. Peter and St. Paul, Apostles

June 29

Great God, under whom we live and whose temples we are, enable us like Your servant Peter, the Rock, to make a good confession of our faith in Jesus, the Christ, and like Your servant Paul, apostle to the Gentiles, to express our faith in word and deed that the gathering of Your scattered sheep may be accomplished before the sounding of the end-time trumpet; through Jesus Christ, our Lord, who with the Father and the Holy Spirit are one God with dominion over us forever.

St. Mary Magdalene

July 22

Risen and reigning Lord, who suffered and died on the cross for the sin of the world, grant us such appreciation of our forgiveness that we hold You in the same devotion as did Mary of Magdala until at last we come into glory where with all the saints we may honor and adore You face to face; who with the Father and the Holy Spirit are one God with dominion over us forever.

St. James the Elder, Apostle

July 25

Holy Spirit, Lord of the church and Champion of its people, lead us into service born of faith and love in Christ, our Redeemer; for then, should we be called to martyrdom because of it, we can walk in the procession of noble witnesses led by Your vanguard servant Jesus; through Jesus Christ, our Lord, who with You and the Father are one God with dominion over us forever.

Mary, Mother of Our Lord

August 15

Eternal Father, whose love encompasses the world, we stand in awe and wonder at the plan for our salvation that included the Virgin Mary, most blessed of all women, through whom Your Son was manifested in our flesh for our salvation; through Jesus Christ, our Lord, who with You and the Holy Spirit are one God with dominion over us forever.

St. Bartholomew, Apostle

August 24

Eternal Lord, Prophet, Priest, and King, who in the days of Your tabernacling among us gathered disciples about You, for the honored place they occupy even now, especially for Your servant Bartholomew, to whom You have fulfilled Your promise, we praise You even as we await the promise of glory which You have made to us who remain faithful unto death; who with the Father and the Holy Spirit are one God with dominion over us forever.

Holy Cross Day

September 14

Lord Jesus, Son of God, who, bowing to the Father's will, endured the Father's judgment against us, we bow humbly before Your cross, for by it we who are sinners are made saints; and we would hold it high, for by it alone sainthood is possible for all sinners; who with the Father and the Holy Spirit are one God with dominion over us forever.

St. Matthew, Apostle and Evangelist

September 21

Blessed Spirit, one with the Father and Son, who elected Matthew to the Kingdom, called him to the faith, inspired him to record the Good News of Jesus Christ, made him an evangelist to his generation, and brought him to eternal sainthood, we say our gratitude to You for all who through his Gospel You have added to the church of Jesus Christ, and pray that by Your power many more be called by the Gospel and won for discipleship; through Jesus Christ, our Lord, who with You and the Father are one God with dominion over us forever.

St. Michael and All Angels

September 29

Almighty God, under whose dominion are all creatures great and small, and all the spirits, good and evil, of the unseen world, hasten the day when St. Michael and all the holy angels will gather the believers in Christ to their eternal home; through Jesus Christ, our Lord, who with the Father and the Holy Spirit are one God with dominion over us forever.

St. Luke, Evangelist

October 18

Holy Spirit, who willed that Your servant Luke should search the sources and examine the records of the Son of God made flesh to fulfill the Law and the Prophets, bless all who hear and read his inspired words with faith in Christ, the Redeemer, that the prayers of Your servant and our prayers for the salvation of souls might be accomplished; through Jesus Christ, our Lord, who with You and the Father are one God with dominion over us forever.

St. Simon and St. Jude, Apostles

October 28

Holy Spirit, blessed Counselor, sent by the Father in the name of our Christ to bring to remembrance the deep truths of God, as Your disciples and apostles Simon and Jude had point and purpose in life because they were with Jesus, so let us who are in Jesus find point and purpose in our lives in Him above all else; through the same Jesus Christ, our Lord, who with You and the Father are one God with dominion over us forever.

Reformation Day

October 31

Ascended Lord, who as Word came to dwell among us, that we might know the love of the Father, lead us ever deeper into the Scriptures—under the blessed guidance of the Holy Spirit—that we learn again and again of the freedom from sin and the Law that Your Gospel has brought us, and that we increase more and more in the life lived to Your Glory through willing service to our fellowman; who with the Father and the Holy Spirit are one God with dominion over us forever.

Collects for
Special Occasions

For the Presence of God

Holy Spirit, who moves the hearts of Your people to praise and thanksgiving, since we are come together into this place of worship to offer gratitude and glory for God's endless gifts to us, we bid Your presence among us, together with the presence of Jesus Christ, our Redeemer, and the heavenly Father, who created and sustains us; through Jesus Christ, our Lord, who with You and the Father are one God with dominion over us forever.

For the Community (Unity)

Lord of lords, Jesus Christ, our Righteousness, whose will it is for all to dwell together in unity, and who in the sacrifice of Your body and blood made us at one with God, grant each of us anew the blessing of the Holy Spirit and faith that works by love, that our community may more nearly match Your dream for it; who with the Father and the Holy Spirit are one God with dominion over us forever.

For the Community (Its Shape)

Holy Spirit, in whose province is the shaping of the community gathered about Christ, constrain us each to accept ourselves as sinners who have come to Christ for peace, and help us to give thanks for those who share the same forgiving love and the same promises of Christ as we, that our community may have the shape You will for it; through Jesus Christ, our Lord, who with You and the Father are one God with dominion over us forever.

For the Community (Mutual Edification)

Holy Spirit, who in the Scriptures consigns us all to sin that the Father might have mercy on us all, help us to communicate the whole consolation of God (the admonition, the kindness, and the severity) to each other, that we be edified, cleansed, and strengthened as members of Christ and as a community of God's people; through Jesus Christ, our Lord, who with You and the Father are one God with dominion over us forever.

For the Christian Community (Solidarity)

Holy Spirit, who has called us by the Holy Gospel and gathered us into a community in Jesus Christ, help us to acknowledge, understand, and appreciate our differences as gifts we bring to each other, lest we use our pride and our brothers' uniqueness to fragment or diminish in any way the gathering You have here called into being; through Jesus Christ, our Lord, who with You and the Father are one God with dominion over us forever.

For the Community (Mutual Burden Sharers)

Holy Jesus, who on the cross bore our griefs, our sorrows, and our punishment, let Your example be always before us that we in love bear with our brothers and sisters, as fellow-redeemed sinners, and willingly share in their burdens as graciously as You have done and do for us; who with the Father and the Holy Spirit are one God with dominion over us forever.

For the Community (Servanthood)

Lord Jesus, who became a Servant willing to suffer death in our stead, give us a sincere desire to so serve those with whom we have to do that the community into which You have placed us may profit from our presence in it; who with the Father and the Holy Spirit are one God with dominion over us forever.

For the Community (Against False Piety)

Holy Spirit, who adorns the whole Christian church on earth as a bride for Christ, restrain us from being falsely pious individuals and a falsely pious community, for very fear of despising our redemption by Christ, our Center, and constrain us to know ourselves and each other as sinners made saints only in Christ, our Lord; who with You and the Father are one God with dominion over us forever.

154

For God's Presence with Us

O Lord God, it it good for us to be here, but now as in the strong name of Jesus we set our faces to the purposes of the holy church, trembling, be with us in the world, that we neither falter in our allegiance to You nor in the ministering to all who are in need of our service; King of kings, hear us, who with the Father and the Holy Spirit are one God with dominion over us forever.

For Servanthood

Holy Spirit, Curator of the holy church and Sanctifier of our lives, use us, earthen vessels that we are, as servants of Christ in the church and in the family of man; for we would follow the example of Christ who was Servant of us all, that the Father may be glorified by our devotion and by all to whom we minister; through Jesus Christ, our Lord, who with You and the Father are one God with dominion over us forever.

For Servants to the Community

Holy Spirit, who distributes talents and gifts and who uses them at will to meet the needs of time and place, we gratefully accept the servant-leaders You have given us, we honor them as your choice for the Kingdom needs of this day, and we pray Your blessing on them as they strive to meet the requirements of their place and position in our community; through Jesus Christ, our Lord, who with You and the Father are one God with dominion over us forever.

For Worship in Servanthood

Almighty God and Father, who has loved us mightily in Jesus Christ, accept our worship of thanksgiving and praise in our gathering this day, and help us to worship in our dedicated service to You as we minister to our neighbor's needs when we are separated from each other; through Jesus Christ, our Lord, who with You and the Holy Spirit are one God with dominion over us forever.

For Thanksgiving for Our Country's Pioneers

Lord Jesus Christ, Ruler of the affairs of mankind, for the fearful people who settled our land when it was new, and who established the principles by which we still seek to govern ourselves, we tender thanks to You and pray for fearless men and women who will continue to contend for our way of life under God with the kind of freedom that we cherish; who with the Father and the Holy Spirit are one God with dominion over us forever.

For the Patriots

Lord of our history, who calls men to match the testing time, we praise You for the fearless men who stood guard and ground at the birth travail of our beloved country, and we pray that their stand for freedom and liberty never be lost to us lest we become again the slaves of tyranny; through Jesus Christ, our Lord, who with the Father and the Holy Spirit are one God with dominion over us forever.

(Adapted from a prayer in
Bicentennial Worship Resources [CPH, 1976], p. 26)

For Our Citizenship

Gracious and benevolent Lord, whose providence is given without bias or prejudice, accept our most sincere gratitude for the country and history into which You have set us, and grant that Your goodness and our gratitude be yet more reason for striving to attain and to maintain the high purpose of our fathers and of our faith in this our land; through Jesus Christ, our Lord, who with You and the Holy Spirit are one God with dominion over us forever.

(From *Bicentennial Worship Resources* [CPH, 1976], p. 24)

For Peace on Earth

Almighty Father, whose angels sang of peace at the advent of Your Son, and who sacrificed that same Son to validate the angelic proclamation, forgive our frightening humanity which struggles so for supremacy at such an awesome price, and help us spread the glorious Word of reconciliation in Jesus Christ, our Savior, with great dispatch to every corner where humanity has not learned it; through Jesus Christ, our Lord, who with You and the Holy Spirit are one God with dominion over us forever.

For the Future

Lord of time, God of eternity, whose divine plan is fixed and whose timetable is rigid, we pray that judgment against the world be stayed until Your dream for peace and concord and Christ's hope for tranquility in the human family be made known, and until many within redeemed humanity say their thanksgiving before Your throne; through Jesus Christ, our Lord, who with You and the Holy Spirit are one God with dominion over us forever.

For Hope

Eternal heavenly Father, who once placed Your Son in a manger, and who set angels to singing over the meadows, and who moved a star across the desert sky, keep hope shining in our dark night and set us to singing on our pilgrimage through time from the cross to the throne where our Savior reigns, King of all kings and Lord of every nation; through Jesus Christ, our Lord, who with You and the Holy Spirit are one God with dominion over us forever.

In Celebration of Certain Saints in Glory

Lamb of God, in whose blood the robes of the saints are washed white to gleaming, and through whom they reign in glory even now, we offer thanks for the gift of eternal life given to Your servants _____, _____ and pray that we may follow their example of faith, that we may be ready and eager to come to You when the distant trumpet blows to summon us; who with the Father and the Holy Spirit are one God with dominion over us forever.

In Celebration of Those Who Have Died in Christ

Gracious Father, who in Jesus Christ, Your Son, have opened the kingdom of heaven to all who believe, we are indebted to You beyond words for Your grace and mercy in Jesus Christ, our Lord, under whom our loved ones whom You have taken to Yourself lived and through whom they have been given eternal life in the mansions You have made ready for Your holy people; through Jesus Christ, our Lord, who with You and the Holy Spirit are one God with dominion over us forever.

For All People

God of all gods, Lord of all people, who by virtue of creation holds dominion over all of us, maintain and sustain the hearts of all who know and acknowledge You as Lord, break open and claim the hearts of all who follow other gods, and in Your patience, love, and power grant us all Your continual benediction; through Jesus Christ, our Lord, who with You and the Holy Spirit are one God with dominion over us forever.

For Thanksgiving for Seedtime and Harvest

Lord of the seedtime and harvest, who set all living things in motion and who maintains them in constant care, we are grateful for the life-sustaining gifts we receive from Your hand each day, praying that there be always enough to supply the needs of the whole human family until the end of time; through Jesus Christ, our Lord, who with You and the Holy Spirit are one God with dominion over us forever.

For Evangelism

Eternal Father, who sent Your Son to redeem our sinful world, and who in turn has commanded us to be in mission, forgive all indifference in us that allows any fellowman to die without a confrontation with Christ, and make and keep us always mindful of our sent-ness, to the glory of Your Kingdom and the honor of Your name; through Jesus Christ, our Lord, who with You and the Holy Spirit are one God with dominion over us forever.

For the Lighting of the Paschal Candle

God of gods, Light of lights, whose radiance dispels all darkness in glory and who is Light on our way through time, keep us always mindful of Your presence in us and among us that the awful darkness of temptation and sin, the lowering dusk of sickness and sorrow, and the gathering night of our last hours be lighted by Your radiant splendor; and in the assembling of ourselves together in Your name keep us conscious of Your blessed nearness to us that we may become light in Your light once more; who with the Father and the Holy Spirit are one God with dominion over us forever.

For Guidance in a Call Meeting

Holy Spirit of the living God, into whose care the affairs of the holy church have been placed by our Lord Jesus Christ, guide us in this hour when we would select a pastor for this place, that one should be sent to us who will meet our needs as a community and a congregation as You see and know them; through Jesus Christ, our Lord, who with You and the Father are one God with dominion over us forever.

For an Anniversary Memorial

Holy Spirit, by whose power and plan the church is strengthened and extended, we, who have this day established this memorial to mark the past year of our history, now ask You to bless its use for the kingdom of Christ and to guide and bless us as we move into our future history; through Jesus Christ, our Lord, who with You and the Father are one God with dominion over us forever.

For an Anniversary

Heavenly Father, from whom neither our yesterdays nor our tomorrows are hidden, keep us conscious of all our gifts of the past, accept our praise this day, and hold Your great wings steady over us, as persons and as a people, as we move into our future; through Jesus Christ, our Lord, who with You and the Holy Spirit are one God with dominion over us forever.

For a Wedding

God of grace and love, under whose dominion we live and upon whom we are altogether dependent, hallow the marriage of these Your children, that grace like Yours be the foundation for it and love like Yours abound in it, to Your honor and glory and for their unity and contentment; through Jesus Christ, our Lord, who with You and the Holy Spirit are one God with dominion over us forever.